C++

Programming

The ultimate beginners guide to effectively design, develop, and implement a robust program step-by-step

MARK REED

Table of Contents

Introduction

This object oriented programming course in C++ language presents learners with the concepts and techniques necessary to effectively design, develop and implement a robust program model. As a learner, you will be able to grasp practical knowledge on how to apply the fundamental concepts of object oriented analysis and design and solve various problems in your day to day activities.

You will learn how to apply the concept of data abstraction, encapsulation, inheritance and polymorphism when creating objects. You will be in a position to create classes that define an object and its behaviour, create objects from a class definition and also be able to establish communication between the objects. You will also learn how to apply the object oriented concepts in performing various tasks and the benefits of doing do.

This book will help you to understand function definition and declaration, how to pass arguments to the function and how to call both inline functions and member functions. Class and objects are an important feature in C++ programming and knowing how to create class definitions and declaring objects as instance of a class will make your program development process easier.

We will teach you to understand the concept of inheritance and polymorphism. You will be able to understand the importance of code reusability and how it makes your work more efficient. In the related chapter, you will learn various ways that inheritance is achieved and how to declare private, public and protected members in a class. Through the inheritance feature, you will be able to implement the concept of polymorphism.

Constructors and destructors is also another important concept in the C++ development framework. This tutorial will enable you to understand how to declare constructors and destructors. you will also be able to work with function uploads and managing dynamic data using the concept of constructors and destructors.

All programs created are stored in the disk drive and knowing how to manage file operations and handling the input/output system will make your work more effective. In this course, you will learn how to use various C++ streams, class streams, and how to use manipulators in managing input and output data. You will also be in a position to open an existing file, write into the file, and read from the file.

You will also be able to detect file errors using various error handling functions. At the end of the course, you will learn about exception handling mechanisms and how to use throw and catch errors techniques.

Chapter One:
Getting Started With C++ Programming

C++ is one of the most competitive general-purpose programming languages on the market. It has features of imperative programming paradigm and can operate in any platform.

Object Oriented Fundamentals

Object oriented programming (OOP) in C++ language revolves around data created using objects. Objects are real-time entities that represent data and methods or functions used in the manipulation of the data.

C++ language uses objects to execute programs. As the program is executed, objects communicate with each other through passing messages. Each object doesn't have to know the implementation details of another object.

C++ utilizes features of OOP to execute a program. The main key features include:

- Objects.

- Classes.

- Data abstraction and encapsulation.

- Inheritance.

- Polymorphism.

A true OOP language uses objects to represent data in any program. Although C++ supports all the OOP features, it is said to be a partial OOP language for the following three reasons:

1. Uses global variables

C++ supports the concept of global variables. You can declare global variables outside of a class so that other entities of the program can access the variables. Though declaring global variables violates encapsulation concept, C++ can support encapsulation through the use of classes and objects.

2. Optional creation of classes or objects

The main function is a mandatory feature in any C++ program and it should be created outside of the class. Therefore, it's not necessary to create classes or objects as long as you have the main ().

Omitting classes or objects violates OOP language concept in that data is represented in the form of objects.

3. Supports friend function

C++ allows you to create a friend class or function that enables you to access the protected members or private members of a certain class. This violates the features of OOP language.

Even though C++ supports the above features, it is referred as a partial object oriented programming language because it sometimes works against the features.

Programming Paradigms

A programming paradigm is a programming model that uses distinct concepts to shape how programmers design, organize and write a program. Programming paradigms are aimed at solving certain problems using various programming languages.

There are different types of paradigms and each fulfils a specific function based on the programming language. These paradigms are divided into two: declarative programming paradigm; and imperative programming paradigm.

Programming Paradigms

Imperitive Programming Paradigm	Declarative Programming Paradigm
Procedural programming Paradigm	Logic Programming Paradigm
Object Oriented Programming	Functional Programming
Parallel Processing Approach	Database Processing Approach

Declarative Programming Paradigm

A declarative programming paradigm is divided into three components: logic; functional; and database or data driven. Declarative programming expresses program logic without focusing on the control flow of the program. The programs developed focus on what to do rather than how to do it. These paradigms emphasize what action needs to be done and declares the results to be achieved. For example, expressing computations include:

Logic programming paradigm

This programming paradigm focuses on solving logical computation problems like a program to solve a puzzle or series of data. Logic programming paradigm relies on the knowledge base which is already known and passes it to a machine learning tool to produce results. The logic paradigm relies on artificial intelligence and machine learning to solve problems.

Functional programming paradigm

This is a language independent program and has its roots in mathematical functions. The main principle in this paradigm is execution of mathematical functions. Data is coupled into functions which hides the implementation details. The functions can be replaced with values and this doesn't change the meaning of the program.

Database or data driven programming paradigm

This programming paradigm focuses on the use of data and movement. All the program statements are defined using data. It is event driven and provides data operation mechanisms like file creation, writing into files, updating files and databases, producing queries and reporting. There are a variety of programs developed for database applications, like the Structured Query Language (SQL), among others.

Imperative Programming Paradigm

Imperative programming paradigm uses a step by step process to achieve a specific goal. It emphasizes how to do a particular task like how to execute several statements and store the results. The paradigm works through change of program state by assigning statements.

Advantages:

- Simple to implement

- Uses loops, variables, functions, and structures to execute program statements

Disadvantages:

- Complex programs increase the complexity of this paradigm

- Parallel programming is not possible in this paradigm

- Less efficient and productive

The imperative paradigm has three broad categories: procedural; parallel processing; and OOP.

Procedural paradigm

Just as the name suggests, this paradigm focuses on step by step processes for performing specific functions. It allows code reusability and it is very easy to implement. It is used to solve simple problems.

11

Parallel processing paradigm

In this type of paradigm, program instructions are processed using multiple processors. A parallel processing paradigm has several processors aimed at running a program in the shortest time possible. Some C++ library functions support this technique.

Object oriented programming (OOP)

This uses a collection of classes and objects to write a program. An object is the smallest entity where all computations takes place. The paradigm focuses on the use of data rather than procedures to solve real world problems. OOP slips the problem into a number of entities represented by objects and then builds data and functions based on these objects. It can solve complex problems about real life scenarios. C++ is a good example of OOP that attempts to eliminate some of the disadvantages of conventional programming languages.

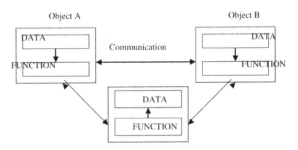

Each of the objects work independently and they're encapsulated within modules. Objects communicate with each other through 'message passing technique'. These objects are organized into several classes in which they can inherit methods and variables needed to perform certain functions such as:

- Advantages.

- Improved data security.

- Code reusability.

- Ability to use inheritance.

- Data abstraction.

Object Oriented Development Framework

Object Oriented Paradigm

An object oriented paradigm relies heavily on system theory as part of its conceptual background. A system represents a collection of entities that interact together to achieve a common objective. These entities may include an individual, an object or an equipment, and abstract entities such as data files and functions.

Object oriented paradigm focuses on objects that encapsulate data and procedures. These objects play a major role in the software development process.

Object Oriented Analysis

Object oriented analysis (OAA) involves techniques used in determining the software requirements of an object, its behavior and interactions. Object oriented design converts the software OOA requirements into specifications for the objects and generates a class

13

hierarchy for object creation. Object oriented programming (OOP) implements the program using objects using OOP language like C++.

Developing program specifications ensures there is a clear and well organized statement of the project problem.

Object-oriented Notation and Graphs

The graphical notation is very important in project design and development processes. These notations represent objects, classes, subclasses and their inter-relationships. The common graphical notations include:

- Instances of objects.

- Message communication between objects within a class.

- Inheritance relationships.

- Hierarchical chart.

- Client-server relationship.

- Classification relationship.

Object oriented analysis provides us with powerful mechanisms to identify objects which are used as the building blocks in the development of the software. Analysis involves decomposition of the software problem into various component parts. It then establishes a logical model which evaluates the system functions.

Steps in object oriented analysis:

1. Identifying the project problem.

2. Creation of a requirement specification document for the users and the software itself.

3. Identifying the project objects and their attributes.

4. Identify what services each object is to perform.

5. Establishing communication between the objects. Objects should be able to interconnect with each other and exchange messages.

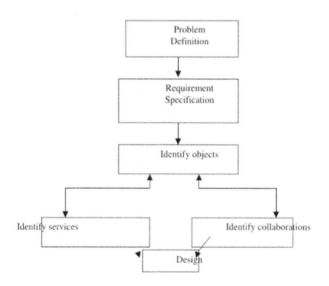

Problem definition

This is the first step in the system development life cycle. It involves understanding the problem the user is facing and writing a problem statement. The problem statement should be refined and redefined using computer system engineering. A well-defined problem statement enables the programmer to come up with a requirement specification document for both the user and the software.

Requirement specification

After clear definition of the problem, you need to understand the objectives of the proposed system and what it's supposed to do. This will help you to generate the system requirements and user requirements in the proposed system.

The requirement specification document should state:

- The outputs which are required.

- The processes to be used to in order to produce these outputs.

- The inputs required.

- The resources required to achieve desired results.

Object identification

This step involves the identification of real world objects and abstract objects. These objects can be found in the application and are analyzed by the use of data flow diagrams (DFD) and textual analysis (TA).

16

Data flow diagrams

A data flow diagram uses various symbols that represent data, and they are used to indicate the flow of data from one point to another. The DFD has input/output symbols, decision symbol and the process symbol which acts as the data store for all objects.

Textual analysis

This includes a detailed textual description of the problem with one or two paragraphs or several sentences based on the complexity of the problem.

1. Identify object services: Once objects are identified, the next step is to determine the set of services each object is supposed to perform.

2. Establish a connection between objects: After determining what services each object will offer, a communication is established between objects based on the services each object offers and receives. You can use an entity relationship diagram or information flow diagram to list information being communicated by each object.

Object Oriented Design

The design process involves mapping out objects and creating a conceptual model of the system. This uses a bottom-up approach to build the system structure, or uses a top-down approach by designing the class member function that provides the services to the system.

When designing objects, it's important to come up with class hierarchies, identify any abstract class and the simply messaging passing process between the objects.

When mapping out content, put into consideration the reusability of classes if you had previous designs, and the classification of the objects into subsystems.

Steps in object oriented design:

1. Evaluate objects created during the analysis phase.

Evaluating the objects identified in the problem space enables you to refine the objects based on their attributes and their operations. It also enables you to identify other objects that can help you obtain more solutions to the problem.

2. Specify class dependencies.

Analysis of the relationship between the classes is very important, as it enables you to determine the appropriate class to represent the objects and establish relationships between the objects. The major relationships necessary in the design stage include:

- **Inheritance relationship:** This allows a class to inherit the properties and behaviors of another class. In this case, an object can inherit some members from another class.

- **Containment relationship:** In this type of relationship, an object of Class A is used as a member of Class B.

- **Use relationship:** This type of relationship provides information on the various classes a particular class uses and how it uses the classes. For example, Class A can use Class B and C in the following ways:

  ○ Class A reads the members of Class B.

  ○ Class A calls the members in Class C.

  ○ Class A uses new operator to create Class B.

If you're planning to override some attributes or functions, it is highly recommended to use an inheritance relationship.

3. Organize classes into hierarchies.

After creating an inheritance relationship between the objects, you have to re-examine the relationships and create class hierarchies. This allows you to reuse data and functions that have been established. Identifying similar attributes and function within a group of related classes helps in organizing the classes into hierarchies. A new class can be formed from the related classes, and it's called the super class. The other classes are subordinate classes. If an object is created by combining all the class attributes, then it's called an abstract class.

19

4. Design classes.

This step defines the methods to be used on the created class to make it more useful. Some of the functions used in a class include:

- **Management functions:** How to create an object and how to destroy an object.

- **Implementation function:** The operations performed on the class data types.

- **Access functions:** This is a function of accessing the internal variables of a class.

- **Utility function:** This involves how to handle errors and access control.

5. Design class member functions.

Member functions define some of the tasks to be performed on an object. These functions work like other normal functions. You can use a top-down function decomposition approach to design member functions.

6. Determine the driver program.

The main() function is the standard C++ driver program. All function calls are made in the main() function. The driver program is responsible for:

- Receiving users' input.

- Creating objects from a class definition.

- Displaying program output based on the users' requirements.

- Making calls to the member functions.

Program Implementation

This process involves coding and testing the developed program. The program code is written using class member functions and the driver program. Once you finish coding the program, you have to test it for errors and to determine whether it functions as expected.

Program testing is an essential feature in the software development process. You should come up with a detailed testing plan of what to test and how the testing will be carried out. Test all the class dependencies and interfaces for any errors. The ultimate goal of program testing is to ensure the program performs its functions as intended.

C++ Programming Building Blocks

Built-in Data Types in C++

When declaring variables, you have to define the data type for each variable. The data type indicates what kind of data is stored in the variable. In C++ programming, the compiler allocates memory space for each variable created based on the data type. Different data types require different memory sizes.

Data Types

There are three C++ data types:

1. Primitive data types

2. Derived data types

3. Abstract or user defined data types

Primitive data types/ built-in data types

A primitive data type is a predefined or built-in data type that is used directly to declare a variable. The most common built-in data types include:

Data Type	Keyword	Range
Character	Char	-127 to 127 and from 0 to 255
Integer	Int	-2147483648 to 2147483647
Floating point	Float	+-3.4e +/-38(7 digits)
Boolean expression	Bool	Stores value as either true or false
Double floating point	Double	+/-1.7e +-308(15 digits)
Valueless	Void	Indicates no type
Wide character	Wchar_t	1 wide character

Character and integer data types can be modified further using the following C++ modifiers:

- Signed

- Unsigned

- Short

- Long

These modifiers indicate how much memory space is needed to store these variables.

Specifying the data type for all variables created tells the compiler how much space to allocate for each variable. Any variable definition specifies the data type and the variable list.

Syntax

Datatype Variable_list;

Example:

int a, b, c;

char y, n;

float salary;

23

Derived data type

As the name suggests, this data type is derived from the built-in data types. They include:

- Arrays.

- Pointers.

- Functions.

- Reference.

Abstract data types

This is a data type defined by the user, thus the name user-defined types. These data types include:

- Enumeration.

- Structure.

- Union.

- Class.

<u>*Enumerated types*</u>

Enumerated data types use 'enum' variable to declare an optional data type and a list of identifiers that show the values of the data type.

Enum enum_name {list of names}

Where,

24

the enum_name is the enumeration data type name. You can have one or more lists of names separated by commas.

For example, we can define an enumeration for class rectangle and call it rectangle and pass variable l to be assigned to length.

Enum rectangle {length, width} l=length;

Variable Scope

A variable is declared either inside a function (local variables) or outside a function (global variables).

Local variables: Defined variables within a block or inside a function are known as local variables. Once declared, only statements within the functions can execute or access the variables.

Example:

```
#include <iostream>

using namespace std;


int main ()

{

  // Declaring local variables:
```

```
int x, y;

int Z;


// Initialization of variables

x = 20;

y = 15;

Z = x - y;


cout << Z;


return 0;

}
```

Global variables: Global variables are declared outside the function and can be called or accessed by any function. The variables are usually declared at the top of the program after the namespace library thus making it accessible throughout the entire program.

Example:

```
#include <iostream>

using namespace std;

// Declaring global variables
```

```cpp
int m;

int main ()
{
    // Declaring local variables:
    int x, y;

    // Initialization of variables
    x = 5;

    y = 10;

    m= x + y;

    cout << m;

    return 0;
}
```

C++ Arrays

If you have multiple variables to store values, you can create an array that allows you to declare a single variable instead of declaring individual variables for each value. An array is a data structure that stores a collection of variables of the same data type.

Arrays are accessed through the use of an index. Each array element is made of contiguous memory allocation with the lowest memory address allocated to the first element of the array, and the highest memory address allocated to the last element.

When declaring an array, you have to specify the data type, array variable name, and the number of elements to be stored in that array variable.

Syntax

Type ArrayName [ArraySize]

This type of an array is a single-dimension array. Type is the data type of the array element and ArraySize must be an integer number that is greater than 0. For example, to declare an array with 3 elements, you can write it as follows:

String cars [3];

Initializing Arrays

You can initialize the arrays created by allocating values to the array elements. These values are added inside braces { } and they shouldn't be larger than the number of elements declared between the square brackets [ ].

Syntax

Type ArrayName [size] = {Values}

Example:

String cars [3] = {"BMW", "RAV4", "Volvo"};

If you want to create an array for integer numbers, you can write:

int num[5] = {5, 10, 25, 20, 35};

Declaring the array size tells the compiler to create a memory allocation to hold 5 elements. If you don't specify the array size, a huge chunk of memory is created to hold the initialized variables.

Arrays use index to represent variables with 0 index representing the first element. You can represent the above array as follows:

Index	0	1	2	3	4
num	5	10	25	20	35

Accessing Arrays

You can access array element by indexing the array name. This can be done by placing the index number of the element you want to access within the square brackets after the array name.

Example:

```
int num[5] = {5, 10, 25, 20, 35};

cout<< num[1];
```

```
// output 10
```

Using Loops in Arrays

You can use for loop to execute array elements.

Example:

```
#include <iostream>

#include <string>

using namespace std;


int main()

{
```

30

```cpp
string cars[3] = {"BMW", "RAV4", "Volvo"};

for(int a = 0; a < 4; a++)

{

        cout << cars[a] << "\n";

}

return 0;

}
```

// output

BMW

RAV4

Volvo

Multi-dimensional Arrays

Multidimensional is an array of arrays which stores data in the form of tables with both rows and columns (rows*columns), also known as the matrix. It can be either a two-dimensional or three-dimensional array.

Syntax

Type ArrayName [Size1] [Size2] ... [SizeN];

Example:

Int M [5] [12];

Int N [2] [2] [3];

To get the number of elements stored in a multidimensional array, multiply the size of all array dimension. In the array of **int M [5] [12]**, you can store (5*12) = 60 elements.

Two-dimensional array

A two-dimensional array is the simplest array format. This array format uses 'r' number of rows and 's' number of columns to form a table. The table ranges from 0 to r-1 for the rows and the from 0 to s-1 for the column number range.

DataType ArrayName [r] [s];

Two-dimension elements in an array are represented by r[x] [y], where 'x' is the row number while 'y' is the column number.

The table below shows a two-dimensional array with three rows and five columns.

	Column 0	Column 1	Column 2	Column 3	Column 4
Row 0	r[0][0]	r[0][1]	r[0][2]	r[0][3]	r[0][4]
Row 1	r[1][0]	r[1][1]	r[1][2]	r[1][3]	r[1][4]
Row 2	r[2][0]	r[2][1]	r[2][2]	r[2][3]	r[2][4]

Example of two-dimensional array:

```
int x [2] [3];
```

You can initialize the array by passing values to the array element as follows:

```
int x [2] [3] = {0, 2, 3, 5, 8, 12}
```

This array can also be initialized as follows:

```
Int x [2] [3] =

{

        {0, 2, 3},

        {5, 8, 12}

        };
```

Example:

```
#include <iostream>

using namespace std;

int main()

{

 int testingarray[3][3] =

        {

        {2, 3, 4},

        {4, 6, 8},
```

```
    {6, 4, 6}



    };

    for(int a = 0; a < 3; ++a)

    {

    for(int b = 0; b < 3; ++b)

    {

    cout<< testingarray[a][b]<<" ";

    }

    cout<<"\n";

    }

    return 0;

}
```

```
// output
```

```
2 3 4

4 6 8

6 4 6
```

Pointers

Pointers are very essential in the implementation of C++ programs. They help in the dynamic allocation of memory space, thus making it easy for the programs to execute efficiently.

When you declare a variable, a memory location is created to store the values. Each of the allocated memory has a defined address which makes it easy to access the variable. Using pointers simplifies program execution by holding the memory address of the stored variable.

A pointer variable points to the data type of the variable and it is created using the asterisk (*) operator. Therefore, before using pointers, you have to declare them.

Syntax

Type *variable-name;

Where,

type is valid C++ data type and variable-name is the pointer variable name.

Example 1: Let's create a pointer named 'ptr' that points to an integer variable.

int *ptr;

When assigning memory address to the pointer variable, an ampersand (&) operator is used.

int *ptr = &variable-name.

Example 2: Create a program that defines a pointer variable and assign memory address to the pointer variable. Add a code to allow the compiler access to the value of the pointer variable in the allocated address.

```
#include <iostream>

using namespace std;

int main ()
{
   int  num = 12;
   int  *ptr;

        // assign memory address to pointer variable
   ptr = &num;

   cout << " The value of the num variable is: ";
   cout << num << endl;
```

36

```
    cout << "The memory address stored in ptr variable is:
";

    cout << ptr << endl;


    cout << " The value of *ptr variable is: ";

    cout << *ptr << endl;


    return 0;

}
```

//output

The value of num variable is: 12

The memory address stored in ptr variable is: 0x28fef8

The value of *ptr variable is: 12

Dynamic Free Store Operators

Free store is unallocated memory dynamically assigned to a program during its execution time. Each program has a large pool of free memory it can utilize during its running time.

All objects allocated to the free store memory require pointers to indirectly manipulate them since the free store memory is unnamed. You also have to manually initialize the free store memory in order to use it.

Dynamic free store memory is manually allocated on the heap while non-static memory with local variables is allocated at the stack.

The allocation of free store memory is via the new operator, and it is deactivated using delete operator. The new and delete operators are system variables available for manipulation by the programmers.

When using data structures like lists and trees, dynamic allocation of free store memory is essential. The new operator is used to request dynamic allocation of free store memory.

Syntax

Pointer= new data-type;

or

Pointer= new data-type [number-of-elements]

Where,

Pointer-variable specifies the pointer of type data type and datatype is any built-in C++ data type.

Number-of-elements is an integer value used when a sequence of several elements or an array of elements is needed. Otherwise, if you only need to allocate free memory for a single element, use **pointer= new type** expression.

Free store objects created using the **new** operator are independent within the scope and are available until destroyed by the **delete** operator.

OOP classes are dynamically allocated free store memory, and they're accessed through the use of pointers and references.

Example:

```
// a pointer initialized with null values

float *ptr = new  float;



// initialize memory using the new operator

int *ptr = new int(15);



// allocation of block memory with an array of 5 integers

int *ptr = new int[5]



// using delete operator for single expression

delete ptr;
```

```
// delete operator for an array of elements

delete[ ] ptr;
```

C++ Functions

A function or method is a group of statements that execute a particular task. C++ functions are divided into two:

1. Library functions

2. User-defined functions

Library Functions

These are pre-defined or built-in C++ functions that perform a number of tasks. For example, main (). You can use the library functions by directly invoking it order to execute an instruction.

Example:

```cpp
#include<iostream>
#include<cmath>
using namespace std;
int main() {
        float num, squareRoot;
        cout<<"Enter a number to get the squareroot:";
        cin>>num;
        squareRoot=sqrt(num);
        cout<<"Squareroot of"<<num<<"="<<squareRoot;
        return 0;
}
```

// output

Enter a number to get the square root: 60

Square root of 60 = 7.74597

The **sqrt()** is a library function used to calculate the square root of a number. While **#include <cmath>** is the header file.

Every C++ program has the **main()** function. For any program to begin its execution, it has to make a system call to the **main()**. That is, the execution starts from the main function.

User-defined Functions

C++ program allow users to define their own functions. A user can specify a function and write a block of statements to be executed once the function is called.

Function Definition and Passing Arguments

Function declaration is very important when defining functions. It tells the compiler about the function name and how to call the function.

Syntax

Type function_name (arguments)

{

Function body/Statements;

}

Where,

Type is the data type returned by the function. If the function executes without any value to be returned after an execution, use void as the return type for the function.

Function_name is the actual name of the function executed.

Arguments or parameter is the value passed to the function. The parameters are optional since a function can have a list of parameters passed to it or not.

Statements or body of the function is a block of statements that explain what the function does.

Example:

```
//function call

float sum (float a, float b)

{

        float sum;

        sum= a+b;

        return sum;

}
```

In the above example, two parameters (**float a,** and **float b**) are passed to function when calling it.

Calling Function

When declaring a function, you have to state what the function will do on the block of statements. To use the declared function, you have to make a call to the function. When the program makes a call to the function, the full control of the program is transferred to that function. As a result, the function executes the defined task under its function body until the end of the function then returns the control back to the main program.

When calling the function, you can pass the parameters needed by the function to execute.

Example:

```cpp
#include <iostream>
using namespace std;
// Declaring Function prototype
float add(float, float);
int main()  {
    float num1, num2, sum;
    cout<<"Enter two numbers:";
    cin >> num1 >> num2;
    // call to the Function
    sum = add(num1, num2);
    cout << "Sum = " << sum;
    return 0;  }
// Function definition
float add(float a, float b)  {
    float add;
    add = a + b;
    return add;
}
```

// output

Enter two numbers: 10 6

43

Sum = 16

Function Prototype

If you want to define your own function (user-defined function), you have to do this outside the **main ()** otherwise the compiler will generate an error. The compiler doesn't recognize user-defined functions and their arguments passed through the main function.

To solve this, you can declare a function prototype outside the **main()**. Function prototype is declared without the function body to enable the compiler to know about the user-defined function in the program. In the above example, function prototype is declared as:

float add (float, float);

Therefore, it is important to define a function prototype if user-defined functions exist in the program and they should be defined before the **main ()** function.

Call by Value and Call by Reference

You can pass data to function using either a call by value or a call by reference. In a call by value, the original value of the function argument is not modified, while in call by reference, its original value is modified.

Call by value

In call by value, the passed value is locally stored in the stack memory. If you change the parameters, the changes only apply to the current function only. The value of the variable inside the **main ()** function will not change when you call the function.

Call by value is the most used method of calling functions, and any changes made to the function parameters will not have any effect on the call to that function.

In call by value, only a copy of the value is passed to the function.

Call by reference

When you pass parameters by reference, the original value of the variable changes. Passing arguments by references modifies the original address of the variable. The original address of the variable is modified with the new variables passed to the function.

When you change the value of arguments in a function, it changes the value of the variable both inside and outside of the **main ()** function.

Inline Functions

When you make a call to a function, the function takes some time to execute a block of statements and store the function return values in the predefined memory allocation before transferring the control back to the program. The program control is switched between the function call and function execution.

Sometimes a function call can take more time than the time it takes to execute a task. The switching time between the function call and the function execution time can create an overhead. To solve this problem, C++ programming implements the use of inline function to reduce the overhead time.

Inline functions reduce calling time for small functions. Whenever a call is made to the function, the compiler expands the function and replaces the function with a corresponding code that reduces overhead time on the function call.

Syntax

Inline return-type function-name (parameters)

{

Function body

}

When you insert an inline keyword before the function, it sends a request to the compiler and its not a command. The compiler can decide to decline the request based on the following conditions:

• The function has static variables.

• You're using recursive function.

• The function uses loop control structures like for, while, and do-while.

• You use switch or go-to statements in the function.

46

- There is no return statements and the function return type is not void.

Example:

```
#include <iostream>

using namespace std;


//declaring inline function

inline int area(int l, int w)

{

        return l*w;

}

int main()

{

        cout << "The area of rectangle is: " << area(3, 5) << "\n";

        return 0;

}
```

Inline functions can be used inside classes. Once you define a function inside a class it automatically becomes an inline function and all the restriction of inline function also apply to functions inside the class.

When defining inline function in a class, you have to declare the function inside the class then define it outside the class using the keyword **inline**.

Class Rectangle

{

Public:

int area (int l, int w)

};

Inline int Rectangle:: area(int l, int w)

{

 Return l*w;

}

Data Structures

Data structure is the collection of elements and variables within a single unit. All data elements of different data types need to be processed and stored together under one name. For example, a student's information file should have details about name, school id, contacts, course, class, marks, and grading information.

Structures work the same as arrays, and the only difference is that structures represent a collection of variables of different data types under a single name, while arrays represent a collection of variables of the same data type.

To declare structures, use the keyword **struct** followed by the structure name which is also called a "**tag**". Then define data members or variables inside the open and closing braces ({}). After the closing braces, enter the object name (structure-variables) although this is optional.

Syntax

Struct StructureName

{

  Type MemberName1;

        Type MemberName2;

        Type MemberName3;

        .

        .

} ObjectName;

The struct keyword tells the compiler that a structure is being defined. The object_name allows a user to directly declare an object of structure type, that is, be able to instantiate different objects in a single object.

Example 1:

```
Struct Person

{

        Char FName[15], LName[15];

        Int age, code;

        Float salary;

} Samuel, Anthony, Paul;
```

The above example defines a structure tag called person, and stores variables of different data types together with objects passed to the structure.

Example 2: Creating a structure with an array of 10 objects

```
Struct Products

{

        Char ProdName [20];

        Int weight;

        Float price;

} items [10];
```

How to Access Structure Memories

Once you define and declare structure variables, you can work directly with their members. To access structure members, use the **dot (.)** operator which is also known as the access operator.

The access operator is inserted between the **object_name** and the **member_name**.

Mango. Price;

Initializing Structure Elements

You can initialize the elements of a structure by assigning values to them. You can initialize the elements by using separate assignment statements or using array notation.

For example, if you want to assign value 50 to the price of mango fruit, this can be done as follows:

Mango.price = 50;

When using an array notation, you can initialize the elements as follows:

Type Student = {10, 15.6, 50.0, 'B'};

The array type initialization only works if the structure variable is already defined. The type in the above statement is the data type specifier of the structure student which is declared and initialized simultaneously. All the values assigned to the structure members should be enclosed with open and closing braces.

51

Example:

```
#include<iostream.h>

#include<conio.h>

#include<stdio.h>


struct student

{

        int StudNo;

        char StudName[30], Course [20], class [2];

        float marks[4];

        char grade;

}student_var;


void main()

{

        float sum = 0;

        float average;


        cout<<"Enter student's number: ";

        cin>>student_var.StudNo;

        cout<<"Enter student's name: ";
```

```
cin>>student_var.StudName;

cout<<"Enter student's course: ";

cin>>student_var.Course;

cout<<"Enter student's class: ";

cin>>student_var.Class;

cout<<"Enter student's marks on 4 subjects:\n";

for(int m=0; m<4; m++)

{

        cout<<"Subject "<<m+1<<": ";

        cin>>student_var.marks[m];

        sum = sum + student_var.marks[m];

}

average = sum / 4;

if(average<50)

{

        student_var.grade = 'Fail';

}

else if(average<65)

{

        student_var.grade = 'pass';

}
```

```
        else if(average<80)

        {

                student_var.grade = 'Credit';

        }

        else

        {

                student_var.grade = 'Distinction';

        }


    cout<<"\nStudent Result:\n";

    cout<<"\nStudNo:
"<<student_var.StudNo<<"\t\t\t        Student        Name:
"<<student_var.StudName;

    cout<<"\nCourse:  "<<student_var.Course<<"\t\t\t
Class: "<<student_var.Class;

    cout<<"\nTotal     Marks:    "<<sum<<"\tGrade:
"<<student_var.grade;


    Return 0;


}
// output
```

Enter student's number: 05

Enter student's name: Sebastian Monroe

Enter student's course: Economics

Enter Student's Class: B2

Enter student's marks on 4 subjects:

Subject 1: 68

Subject 2: 74

Subject 3: 86

Subject 4: 94

Students Result:

StudNo: 05   Student Name: Sebastian
Monroe

Course: Economics   Class: B2

Total Marks: 322   Grade: Distinction

References in C++

C++ reference is an alternative name assigned to an existing variable. Once you initialize a variable name with a reference, you may use the variable name or the reference to call a variable.

There are three types of references supported in C++ programming language. They include:

- **Non-constant references:** These are simply called references and are declared to non-constant values.

- **Constant references:** These consist of constant values

- **R-value references:** These help to avoid repetitive copying and assist forwarding functions.

In non-constant references, variables are declared as references using the ampersand (&) operator which is declared between the variable name and the reference type.

```
Int &ref = {value};
```

The ampersand operator in this case will mean 'reference to' and not 'address of'. These references work the same as the values their referencing. That is, it acts as an alias of the referenced object.

Example 1:

```
int prd= {5};

int &x = {prd};

int &y = {x};
```

In the above example, 'x' is a reference to **prd** variable while 'y' is also a reference to 'x'.

Example 2:

```cpp
#include<iostream>

using namespace std;


int main()

{

  double price = 100;


  double &ref = price;


  // change the price to 120

  ref = 120;

  cout << "price = " << price << endl ;


  // now change the price to 150

  price = 150;

  cout << "ref = " << ref << endl ;


  return 0;
```

}

// output

Price = 120

Ref = 150

Application of References

1. **To modify the parameters of a function:** If you want to change the parameters passed to a function during function call, you can reference the variables. In the above example, referencing the variable, modified the price value from the original 100 to 120.

2. **To avoid copying large structures:** If you have a function that executes a large number of objects, then passing parameters to it without referencing them creates a copy of object-variables. This results in wastage of CPU time and memory. To avoid this duplication of objects, you can use references.

Example:

```
Struct Employee

{

  string EmpNames, address;

  int EmpNo;

}
```

```
Void print (const Employee &em)

{

   Cout << em.EmpNames << " " << em.address << " " <<
em. EmpNo;

}
```

If we remove the reference to operator, it will create a new copy of the employee object. The **const** keyword prevents any accidental update to the program.

3. **To modify objects in for each loop:** You can use references to modify all elements in for loop or to avoid copying of objects when working with large objects.

Chapter Summary

C++ is a general purpose programming language and one of the most competitive object oriented programs in the market. The language utilizes features of object oriented programming to design a program and manipulate data. The commonly used features include: objects, classes, data abstraction, encapsulation, inheritance and polymorphism.

With the help of programming paradigms, programmers can easily design, organize and build a program that solves various problems. There are two types of programming paradigm; a declarative programming paradigm and an imperative programming paradigm. C++

language is an imperative programming language since it relies on OOP concepts to execute functions.

The major key elements in this chapter included:

- Learning various built-in data types and how to use them in writing a program.

- How to use user-defined types to execute complex programs.

- How to declare variables in C++ and allocate memory location for the user variables.

- How to declare arrays to hold data elements, initializing arrays, accessing array elements as well as know how to work with both two dimensional arrays and multidimensional arrays.

- Using pointers to point to a specific storage location and allow you to determine the reference address of the variable.

- Learning how to use dynamic free store operators to allocate memory space for your programs.

- How to use C++ functions to build programs and implement code reusability features to make complex programs more effective.

- Learn function definitions, how to declare functions, make function calls, and how to use function prototypes and inline functions.

- Learning how to use references when dealing with large objects to enable you reduce the overhead time in function calls. References will help you minimize CPU execution time and save on memory space since it prevents duplication of objects whenever a function call is made.

- How to use structures and references to access objects. Data structures allow you to work with variables of different data types under a single unit.

- Creating variables with different return types and data elements under a single name to avoid code repetition.

- Making calls to structure functions and pass arguments of different data types.

In the next chapter you will learn basic concepts of object oriented programming including the use of classes, objects, data abstraction and encapsulation, polymorphism and inheritance feature.

Chapter Two:
Basic Concepts in Object Oriented Programming

It is necessary to understand the basic concepts used in object-oriented programming. See figure below.

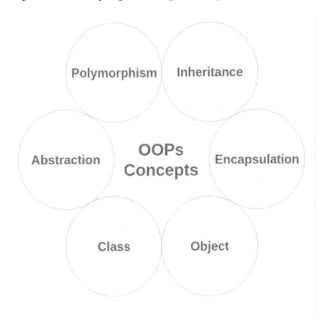

Class

A class is an expanded concept of data structure and a building block for C++ programming language. It consists of logical methods for organizing data and functions in the structure. The 'class' keyword denotes the data structure with functions represented as members.

A class consists of two parts: class header and body. A class header defines the class name and the base class, whereas the class body defines the class members supported by each class. The class uses user-defined data type to hold its own data members and member functions. Class members and functions are accessed by creating an instance of the class.

Class members: They represent the data variables in that class and specify how class objects are represented.

Member functions: Describes the function prototype used in manipulating these data variables. It specifies class operations which is also referred to as the instance of the class.

Both member functions and data members define the properties and behavior of an object in a class.

Class members fall under three access permissions: public, private and protected.

Public members: Data members in this class are accessible by every class member and from anywhere as long as the class is visible.

Private members: In this class, data members are only accessible by the class members or other members of the same class.

Protected members: These are only accessible within the class members and other members from a derived class.

Syntax

Class ClassName

{

Access Specifier:

Member(s);

Access Specifier 2:

Members(s);

Access Specifier n:

Member(s);

};

Where,

- **Class** is the keyword that denotes class declaration.

- **ClassName** is a valid name identifier of class.

- **Access Specifier** is the access permission granted to that class: either private, public or protected.

- **Members** defines the class members and member functions of the class.

Example:

Class Cars

{

Char CarName[30], brand[30];

Float SpeedLimit, Mileage;

Public:

Void getdata(void);

Void display(void);

};

In this example, the data members will be CarName, brand, SpeedLimit and Mileage. The member function is getdata, display, a function to apply breaks or even a function to increase the speed of the car.

From the above data, we can deduce that a Class is the blue-print that defines a group of objects with similar properties and behaviors.

Objects

In C++, an object is an entity or variable which possess some characteristics and behaviors. It represents an instance of the class. That is, when you define a class, there is no memory allocation but if the class is instantiated (declaring variables), a memory allocated is created and allocated to the specific objects created.

An object can represent a person, a car, or bank account. Objects include both data members and their associated member functions, known as methods.

When creating a class, you have to determine the attributes of the object you're creating, commonly known as the data members of the class. For example, Class Cars (object) has attributes like car model, year of manufacturer, engine power, and color. Its associated member functions or methods include; start(), stop() and move().

You may have more than one instance of the object created. The car objects include: Toyota, Rav4, Fielder, Land Rover, etc.

An instance is an actual object which is created during run time. For example, Toyota is an instance of Class Cars.

To determine the behavior components of the objects, you have to determine what message the objects can receive and what kind of operations need to be performed. The behavior component of the class type object describes a collection of member functions which send a message to the object and prompt a certain action to be taken.

Note: all messages are sent from one object to another by calling or invoking member functions.

Syntax

Identifier. Message ([arg1, arg2])

Where,

- **Identifier** is the object name.

- **Dot** represents the member access operator.

- **Message** is the type of message sent.

- **Arg** is an optional list of arguments to be returned or the message content.

The dot between the identifier and the message type is the member access operator that identifies the data members and member functions of the object.

For example:

```
Class Person

{

    Char FName [25], LName[25];

    Int age;

Public:

    Void getdetails()

    Void display()

};

Void Person :: getdetails()

    {
```

```
Cout<<"Enter your first name and last name";

Cin>>FName, Lname;

Cout<<"enter your age";

Cin>>age;

}
Void Person :: display()

{

Cout<<"Your name
is:"<<FName<<LName<<aged"<<age;

}
Int main()

{

Person P; //P is an object

p.getdetails(); //call to enter names and age function

p.display(); // call to display your names and age

Return 0;

}
```

Objects created generate a memory space for storing data. When you run the above program, the objects interact by sending messages to each other through a **message passing** technique.

68

Each of the objects has data and the code needed to manipulate the data. Objects can send messages to one another without knowing the content of each other's data or the execution code.

The Class Person has two private member attributes (names and age), and public member functions (getdetails() and display()). These functions are declared within the class as the prototype.

The function name is followed by a double colon which identifies getdetails() and display() as function member to Class Person.

If a class is created, the class name defines a new data type called an **object p**.

From the example above, **Person P** is an object created of the Class Person where P sends a call to the function getdetails (P.getdetails();).

When you call this function, the compiler prompts you to enter the first name, last name and the age of the person and store them in the class private members.

P.display() is a call to retrieve the stored data on the names and age of the person.

Data Abstraction

Data abstraction is another important feature in C++ programming. Data abstraction provides needed information without presenting the entire details. It only displays the information needed while hiding the background data details.

Classes helps in implementing abstraction in C++. Using access specifiers, you can group a class based on member functions and data members. This makes it easy to know which data member will be visible to the users and what data remains hidden.

Abstraction can also be applied on header files. For example, when using **pow()** in calculating the power of a certain number you only call the function **pow()** from **math.h header file** and pass the parameters to it. You don't have to know how the functions work on the background, you're only interested in what the function does and the results of the calculation.

Data Encapsulation

Data encapsulation is the process of wrapping data and functions under a single unit called a **class.** That is, wrapping data together with its manipulation methods or functions.

In encapsulation, you can't access data directly. You can only access it via a function inside the class.

When working with data, encapsulation ensures data is not directly accessible and can only be accessed through a function prototype inside a class. This makes the concept of data hiding possible.

For example, if you're an accountant and want to obtain sales data for a particular week, you don't have access to all data in the sales section. You can contact the sales manager in charge of sales section and request him to retrieve sales for a specific week. The sales data and sales manager are wrapped under a single class called 'sales section'.

Encapsulation makes it easy to create the concept of data hiding or data abstraction. For example, hiding data that is not required in the sales class.

Encapsulation in C++

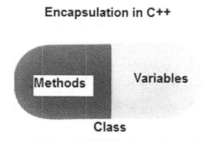

Class

Polymorphism

Polymorphism is representation of data in more than one form. It allows functions and variables of different types to be used at different times. That is, a variable or function can exhibit a different behavior at different instances.

When performing an operation, a simple function call can give different results depending on the data type of the variables passed. Polymorphism allows operators to exhibit different behaviors.

There are two types of polymorphism:

- Operator overloading

- Function overloading

Operator overloading: This is where an operator show different results in different instances.

Function overloading: This is where a single function name performs different types of tasks.

Example: You can write a function to calculate a sum of numbers with different parameters. Create function 1 & 2 and pass two parameters of integer type to the first function, and supply the second sum function with three parameters of integer type. When you make a call to the sum function, it will give different instances. Therefore, polymorphism allows you to use the same method and pass different parameters to it.

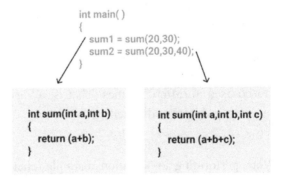

```
int main( )
{
    sum1 = sum(20,30);
    sum2 = sum(20,30,40);
}
```

```
int sum(int a,int b)
{
    return (a+b);
}
```

```
int sum(int a,int b,int c)
{
    return (a+b+c);
}
```

Inheritance

This is a concept where you develop a new class from an existing class or from a base class. The new class derived will have the characteristics of the base class. The base class will act as the parent or super class while the derived class will act as the child class or a sub-class.

The sub-class inherits all the properties and characteristics of the super class (parent class).

Inheritance supports the concept of code reusability. This is very important as it helps in reducing the overall code written to perform a certain task, thus making it a great feature in object oriented programming. If you want to create a new class that uses some of the code in another class, you can derive a new class from the existing class. This allows you to re-use the variables and methods in the existing class.

Other Features

Dynamic Binding

When you make a call to a function, the code to the function is executed at runtime. This process is known as dynamic binding. C++ uses virtual functions to support dynamic binding.

Message Passing

Message passing is a technique in which objects communicate with one another. An object sends a message to another object requesting execution of a certain procedure. This triggers a function in the receiving object to send back the desired results.

When an object is communicating with another object, it has to specify its name, the function name, and the message to be sent.

C++ language supports static message passing, that is, when you invoke an object's method, the target object should also have the invoked method. Otherwise, the compiler will generate an error message. Message passing is made through the help of **vtables**.

To use dynamic message passing on objects, you should:

- Declare a global function that will act as a signature to the message being passed between objects.

- Inherit object properties from dmp::object.

- Create a class constructor and add a single message or more to the object by using add_message method.

- Use invoke(signature, …parameters) to send a message to an object.

How Message Passing Works

Each C++ object has a **shared_ptr** to a particular map. That is the map's key act as a pointer to the message signature. Its value points to an internal message structure that holds the pointer of the message method to invoke.

Once the object method is invoked, it retrieves the appropriate message structure from the map. As a result, it invokes the object method using **this** as the object target.

The objects share the message map among themselves to increase efficiency among themselves. If the map is not unique, it will be duplicated after modification of a message map.

Chapter Summary

In this chapter, you have learned basic concepts of object oriented programming including:

- Learning how to work with C++ objects and initialize them.

- How to create classes and class definition.

- Applying the concept of data data abstraction and encapsulation to extend the power of programming language.

- Learning how programmers can create user-defined data types and how encapsulation and abstraction work in order to provide the needed information to the user without the need to present program details.

- Learning how the concept of data hiding is made possible through encapsulation.

- How to use OOP polymorphism feature to create objects with more than one data type or form.

- How to use function overloading and overloaded operator in polymorphism.

- Learning how C++ supports inheritance feature by allowing the properties and characteristics of a class (base class) be used in building another class (derived class).

- Dynamic binding feature and how message passing works.

In the next chapter you will learn how to build base classes and derived classes as well as how to work with data members and member functions.

Chapter Three:
Working with Classes and Objects

In the previous chapter, you learned about classes as user-defined data type that acts as a blueprint for creating objects. Classes extended the concept of data structures and just like data structures, they have data members and additional member functions.

Using Classes

When working with complex class functions, defining member functions inside the class makes it difficult to manage the class.

Class Headers and Class Body

C++ programming language allows code reuse by putting class definition in the header file. This prompts code reuse in multiple files or projects. Just like declaring functions in the header file so as to use the function in multiple projects, a class definition is put in the header file with the same name as the class.

The member functions of this type of class are defined outside of the class and stored in a **.cpp** file with the same name as the class.

A class header file consists of class definition with its data members and member function prototypes.

Note: Putting all member functions inside the header file may cause clutter in your class definition. All functions defined inside a class are implicitly inline, and if you're dealing with a complex function that is invoked more often, it will slow down the execution time of the function code.

If you change some function code in the header file, then you have to make the same changes in every file that includes the header. Otherwise, it will affect the recompilation process of the project.

But if you change some function code in a .cpp file, you only need to recompile the .cpp file.

Definition and Declaration of Class

In C++, a class consists of related functions and data. Data and functions in a class are combined together to form a data type that is used in creating objects of the type. The classes created represent real world entities made of various data type properties and behavior (that is, their associated operations).

Syntax

Class class-name {

Access-specifier 1:

Member1;

Access-specifier 2:

Member 2;

...

} object-names;

78

Where,

- The class keyword specifier indicates the new data-type and it is followed by the class-name which is the specific name that identifies that class.

- The body of the class is made of both private and public access specifiers.

Private

The private access specifier helps in implementation of data hiding concept. This is achieved by using the keyword **'private'** when declaring member values. The data members and functions declared under the **Private** keyword can only be accessed from within that class itself.

The data hiding concept is a security technique that prevents unauthorized users from performing any data operation like read/write operation or modification of data. Therefore, **Private** data declaration, hides data from unauthorized users and any accidental manipulation.

Public

In public access specifier, both data and functions can be accessed outside the class. Member functions declared in the class are generally public and as a result, you can access them from outside the class.

Class definition for both private and public members is shown below.

Class class-name

{

Private: Variable declaration (data members);

Function declaration (member function);

Public: Variable declaration;

Function declaration;

Protected: Variable declaration;

Function declaration;

};

Syntax

Class mytest

{

Private:

int x;

double y;

```
        string *name;

        void getX () {x=25;}

        ...;

Public:

        int count;

        void getY () {y=15;}

        ...;

};
```

Where,

- In this example, x, y, and the names are defined inside the class thus, they are private members which can be accessed within that class.

- Count is a public data member which can be accessed from anywhere outside the class.

Data Members and Member Function Definitions

Data members are any variables declared in a class using the standard data types like **char, int, float, double**, etc. or using derived data types like **class, pointers**, and **structures**.

A class member function consists of function definition or prototype within the class. The function prototype works on any object of the class it is in and also has access to all other data members in the class. There are two types of member function definition: class; and class method

Class definition

This describes the data members and member functions of the class.

Class methods definition

This describes how a program is to perform certain tasks. It shows how member functions are coded. The member function code can be written in two ways:

- Using **inside class** definition

- Using **outside class** definition by the use of scope resolution operator (::)

In this case, the function code is the same but the function header is different in both cases.

<u>*Inside class definition*</u>

If you define a member function inside the class, there is no need to place the membership label within the function name. To easily implement this, you can use **inline functions**.

When you use inline functions, the compiler inserts the function body code at the specific point where the function is invoked or called. This ensures fast execution of the program.

Example: Creating class rectangle to access the class members using the member function instead of accessing the members directly.

Syntax

Class Rectangle

```
{
    Public:
        Float length;
        Float width;
        Float getArea (void)
        {
            Return length*width;
        }
};
```

Outside class definition using Scope Resolution operator (::)

In this class defines, the function is declared outside the class as demonstrated below.

Syntax

Type class-name:: function-name(parameters)

83

```
{

Function body

}
```

The :: operator allows you to define member functions outside the class. The operator was earlier used to identify a global variable in situations where the global variable had the same name as the local variable.

Example:

```
Class Rectangle

    {

        Public:

            Float length;

            Float width;

            Float getArea (void)

    };

Float Rectangle ::getArea (void)

        {

            Return length*width;

        }
```

To call the member function, you have to use a dot operator (.) as shown in our previous chapter. The dot operator allow you to manipulate data in an object and make a function call to the object.

Syntax

Rectangle rect;   // create a rectangle object

Rect.getArea ();   // make a call to the member
function of the object

Example:

```cpp
#include<iostream.h>
#include<string>
using namespace std;
class product
{
string prd_name;
float weight, price;


public:
void mgetdata()
void mfdisplay ()
```

```
} item;
void product::mfgetdata()

        {

        cout<<"Enter the product name";

        cin>>prd_name;

        cout<<"Enter the product weight and price";

        cin>>weight>>price;

        }
void product::mfdisplay()

        {

        Cout<<"product name is"<<prd_name<<"Weight
is"<<weight<<"and the price"<<price<<endl;

        }
//calling class member functions

int main()

{ product item;

item.mfgetdata();

item.mfdisplay();

return 0;

}
```

To access the private data members, you have to create **getter** and **setter function (mfgetdata()** and **mfdisplay())** in order to get and set the value of the private data members. The setter function sets the value of the parameter passed to the private data member while the getter function returns the value of the private data member that needs to be used. Both getter and setter functions must be defined public.

Using Protected Data Members

In a protected data member function, data members and member functions are used by that current class or by the derived class where they are declared.

You can access protected data members using the dot (.) operator within a subclass of the current class. Just like the public class, you can access protected members from a class, friend function, or from a derived class.

If class members are declared as protected then:

- Only the member functions of the original class that declared it can have access to the variables.

- Only the friends of the class that originally declared the members as protected access class members.

- They are accessed directly by a privately derived class that has private access to the protected members.

87

- Only classes derived with either public or protected access from a class where the data members were originally declared can use them.

When using base classes, then the protected keyword indicates that both the public and protected members of the base class are protected data members of the derived class.

The protected data members are not as private as the private data members or more public than the public data members which can be accessed from any function.

You can declare protected data members as static, meaning they will be accessible to friend function or member function of a derived class. If the members are not static, then they can be accessed in the friend function and derived member functions using pointers or references.

Types of Class Member Functions

There are several member functions which can be utilized to manipulate data members and functions in C++. These special member functions include:

1. Simple functions.

2. Static functions.

3. Const functions.

4. Inline functions.

5. Friend functions.

Simple Member Functions

These are the basic member functions declared in C++. They don't use any special keywords like static as they're prefix. The general format of the basic or simple member functions is shown below.

Syntax

Type function_name (arguments)

{

  Function body;

}

Static Member Functions

These member functions uses keyword **static** and it's associated with both data members and member functions. Static means something that holds the same position.

To make a function static, use the keyword static followed by the function name. Static functions works for the entire class rather than for a specific object of the class.

Static functions are called using object and direct member access operator (.). You can also call static member function using the class name, a scope resolution operator, or by itself.

Syntax:

```
Class S

{

        Public:

        Static void fxn ()

        {…}

};

int main() {

        // call the member function directly with its class
name.

        S::fxn ()

}
```

The above function can only access static data members and static member functions. The ordinary data members or functions can't be accessed.

Const Member Functions

Const keyword is used to declare constant variables. Once a variable is defined as constant, its values can't be changed. When **const** is used with member functions, those functions can't modify the data objects or the related data members.

Syntax

Void x () const

```
{

    // function body

}
```

1. Inline Functions

When you define member functions inside a particular class, the function automatically becomes an inline function.

2. Friend Functions

Friend functions provides private access to non-class functions. These functions are not a class member function. Friend function allows you to declare a global function as a friend or a member function of another class as a friend.

Syntax:

Class friendclass

```
{

        int x;

        Public:

        Friend void fn() //set global function as a friend

];
Void fn()
```

```
{

    Friendclass fc;

    // accessing private data member

    fc.x=10;

    cout<<fc.x;

}
Int main() {

  fn ()

        }
```

A friend function will be able to access the private member function through creation of class objects. You can also make your entire class as a friend class. If you make a class to be a friend class, then all the member functions automatically become a friend function.

Example:

```
class anotherfriendclass

{

    void fn();

};


class Friendclass
```

```
{
    private:

    int x;

    public:

    void getdata();  //


    // make the class function anotherfriendclass

    friend void anotherfriendclass::fn();


    // e complete class as friend

    friend class anotherfriendclass;
};
```

Building Classes

When creating classes, there are two types of classes you can create: base class and derived class.

Base Class and Derived Class

A base class is a class which allows building of other classes from it. That is, it allows other classes to be derived from it. A base class facilitates creation of a new class that reuses the code inherited from the original base class. The derived class inherits both properties and methods of the base class. You can extend the functionality of base class by overriding members in the derived class.

A base class is also called a parent class or super class while the derived class is called child or subclass.

Any class built from the base class inherits both the data and behavior of the base class.

Properties of a base class:

- Base classes are instantiated automatically before building derived class.

- During instantiation, a derived class communicates with base class through calling the base class constructor with similar parameter list.

- Members of the base class are accessed from the derived class by the use of an explicit cast.

- Defining abstract methods in the base class so that the class automatically becomes an abstract class. A non-abstract class from derived class can override data members in the abstract class.

The base class members have private, public, and protected access modifiers where the private members are accessible within the class. Public members are accessed outside the class while the protected members are accessed within the class or by a subclass.

A derived class can only access the public and protected members of the base class. Private members are inaccessible.

Chapter Summary

In this chapter you learned how to use classes to solve various problems, including:

- How to use class headers and class body when defining objects, and how to define and declare classes.

- How to differentiate between data members and member functions.

- How to declare both data members and member function, and determine whether they should be declared as private, public or protected members.

- How to access the private, public and protected members in a class, as well as make calls to the member functions.

- How to work with different class member functions when invoking specific functions.

- How to build classes using the base class and derived classes. From the base class or the parent class, you can derive a child class which inherits the behavior and properties of the base class.

- You will be able to know more detailed information about how the derived class inherits these properties in our next chapter.

In the next chapter you will learn about class inheritance, including how the derived class inherits properties. At the end of the chapter you will be able to derive new classes from an existing class, learn how to apply different types of inheritance to solving problems, identify relationships between classes, learn how to apply inheritance in constructors and destructors, and lastly be able to manage dynamic data.

Chapter Four:
Extending Classes via Inheritance

Deriving New Classes from Existing Classes

Inheritance is an object oriented programming feature that allows a class to borrow the members of other classes without repetition of its members. It allows one class (derived class or subclass) to acquire the properties and methods of another class (base class or superclass). A class whose properties are inherited is called the base, parent or superclass while the class that inherits these properties is called a derived, subclass or child class.

When a class inherits properties of another class, the variables and functions of the base class are available to the new class, hence promoting code reusability. The derived class inherits all members except the private members.

Importance of inheritance:

1. Supports code reusability

2. Support overriding method

3. Uses virtual keyword

Base Class and Derived Class

When inhering members of another class, the public members of the superclass will remain public while the protected members will remain protected. In a private inheritance, both public and protected members of a superclass will remain private in a subclass.

Syntax

Class subclass: access_mode superclass

The superclass should be declared first, that is, before you define the subclass. The access mode (private, public or protected) specifies what superclass properties are to be inherited by subclass.

For example, assume you have a class employee and class manager, where the manager is also an employee who has additional responsibilities. You can apply inheritance concept to avoid repeating data members and member functions in employee class to the manager class.

The manager class can be declared as shown below.

Class Manager: Public Employee

{

Public:

// additional manager member components

...

};

Inheritance helps you declare manager class without repeating those member components inside the employee class. Employee is the base class while manager is the derived class.

```
class student

    {

            char* studname, course;

            int age;

            char* department;

    Protected:

      student(char* studname);

            void display();

    };




    class HOD : Protected student

    {

            studentlist students;


    Protected:

            HOD(char* studname, student* people);

            void display();

    };
```

Types of Inheritance

Single Inheritance

Single inheritance is one of the simplest types of inheritance where a class is derived from a single class. The derived class will inherit member components from only a single class. For example, class B inherits properties and behaviors of class A. Class B inherits both the public and protected members of class A.

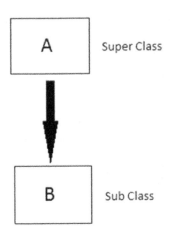

Syntax

Class B: public A {/*...*/};

Or

Class B: Protected A {/*...*/};

Multiple Inheritance

In multiple inheritance, a class can inherit members from two or more direct base classes. For example, you can create derived class C from class A & B base classes.

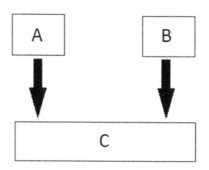

Syntax

Class C: public A, public B {/*...*/};

Example:

#include<iostream.h>

Class Polygon

{

protected:

　　　int width, height;

　　　Public:

　　　void setvalues (int w, int h)

```
        {

        width=w, height=h;

        }

};

Class output

{

public:

        void output (int);

};

void output::output (int i)

{

        cout<<'i'<<endl;

}

class rectangle:public polygon, public output

{

public:

        int area()

        {

        return width*height;
```

102

```
        }
};
class triangle: public polygon, public output
{
        int area()
        {return (width*height/2);}
};
int main()
{
        rectangle rect;
        triangle tri;
        rect.setvalues (6,4);
        tri.setvalues (6,4);
        cout<<        "Area        of        rectangle
is:"<<rect.output(rect.area);
        cout<< "Area of triangle is:"<<tri.output (tri.area);
        return 0;
}
```

Multi-level Inheritance

This is a where a derived class inherits from a class which also inherited properties of another base class. For example, if A is the base class of B while class B is the base class of C, then C will be the derived class of B and B will be a derived class of A.

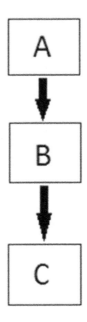

Hybrid inheritance/virtual inheritance

Hybrid is a combination of several inheritance types. For example, class B and C are the derived classes of base class A. From the derived class B and C, you can create a new derived class D. This forms a hybrid inheritance since it combines multiple inheritance types to form a new class.

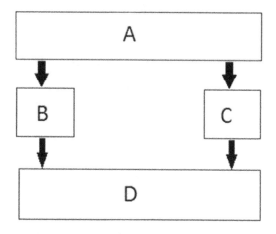

Hierarchical inheritance

Hierarchical inheritance has multiple subclasses which inherit properties of a single base class. Class B, C, and D inherit the properties of single class A.

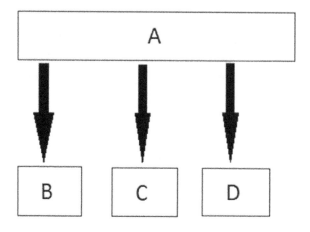

Relationships

C++ supports encapsulation in which data is bundled together with the specific functions that operate on it, thus forming a single unit. This process ensures data is only accessed by functions operating on it and not outside the class. This protects the class member functions from being accessible outside.

To access the private and protected members outside the class, you have to use the special feature called the friend function or class to access the private members. The friend function allows you to access non-public members of a class. That is, a class can allow other non-member functions and other classes to access its private members by making them friends.

To make the private and protected classes accessible, you have to declare a prototype of the external class allowing it to gain access to the private members of another class. The friend keyword is placed on the function declaration of the friend function and not in the function definition. The friend function is invoked without any object since the function has its own arguments as objects.

Syntax

Class class-name

{

...

…

Friend Type Function_name (arguments)

}

 Example:

```
#include<iostream.h>

class square;

class rectangle
{
        int length, width;
public:
        int area()
        {
        return (length*width);
        }
        void convert (square s);
};


class square
{
```

```
private:

        int side;

public:

        void setsize (int a)

        {

        size= a;

        }

        friend class rectangle

};

void rectangle::convert (square s)

{

        length= s. length

   width=s.side;

}


int main()

{

   rectangle.rect

        square. sqr
```

```
    sqr.setvalues (a);

        rect. convert (sqr);

    cout<<rect.area();

        return 0;

}
```

Example 2:

```
#include <iostream.h>

class XYZ

{

private:

    int x, y;

public:

    void text()

    {

        x=50, y=75;

    }

    friend int compute (XYZ E1,E2)

};
```

```
int compute (XYZ E1)

{

    return int (E1.x+E2.y)-5;


}

int main()

{

    XYZ E

    E.test

    cout<< "The result is:"<<compute(E)

    return 0;

}
```

Construction and Destruction of Derived Objects

Constructors and destructors are C++ tools used for creating objects. Constructors initialize member variables in an object while a destructor is used in destroying that object. Whenever an instance of a class is created, it invokes the constructor method.

Constructors use the same name like class and no return type, while a destructor uses the same form of naming as class but it has ᴗ at the beginning of the class declaration.

110

During program execution, the compiler automatically calls the constructor and destructor variables. If the base class has no parameters passed to it, then the derived class doesn't need any constructor. If the base class has a parameter list, then the derived class should have a constructor.

The derived constructor class will pass its arguments to the base class constructor. When using inheritance concept, you can declare objects using the derived class. Once you declare objects in a derived class, the constructor of the base class and derived class are automatically executed.

Constructors and Destructors in Base and Derived Classes

Inheritance of destructor objects execute in reverse order during execution of a constructor. When the object gets out of scope, the destructor is executed. See below for an example of constructor and destructor program using multiple inheritance.

Syntax

```
#include<iostream.h>

#include<constream.h>


class Base1

{
```

```
Public:

base()//constructor with zero arguments

    {

        cout<<"Zero arguments constructor /n";

    }

    ~base()

    {

        cout<<"Destructor of base1 class/n";

    }

};


class Base2

{

    public:

    base2()

    {

        cout<< "Zero argument constructor for base2
class/n";

    }
```

```
        ~base3()

            {

        cout<< "Destructor of base2 class/n";

            }

};


class Base3: Public Base1, Public Base2

{

        public:

        base3()

            {

        cout<<"Zero argument constructor for a derived
class /n";

            }

        ~base3()

            {

        cout<<"Destructor of the derived class /n";

            }

};
```

```
int main ()

{

  clrscr ();

  Base3 obj; //declaring object

  return 0;

}
```

//output

Zero arguments constructor

Destructor of base1 class

Zero argument constructor for base2 class

Destructor of base2 class

Zero argument constructor for a derived class

Destructor of the derived class

In the above program, base1 and base2 are the superclass while base3 is the derived class. The constructors of the superclass are executed first before executing the derived class. The destructor of the derived class is executed before executing the superclass.

114

You can call the superclass constructor in a derived class constructor. When you create a derived class object from an existing base class, the base class becomes a constructor by default, and it is executed first then followed by the derived class.

When making a call to a base class constructor with parameters inside the derived class constructor which also has parameters, then you have to explicitly mention it when declaring the parameters of the derived class constructor.

Base class is the default constructor which is present in all types of classes. See example below.

Syntax

```
class construct

{

        int x;

        public:


    construct()

        {

    cout << "Building default constructor\n";

        }

};
```

115

```cpp
class Child : public construct

{

        int y;

        public:


        Child()

        {

    cout << "Default derived  constructor\n";

        }

        // constructor with parameters

    Child(int z)

        {

    cout << "Parameterized derived constructor\n";

        }

};


int main()

{
```

```
    construct c;

        Child c1;

        Child c2(10);

}
```

//output

Building default constructor

Default derived constructor

Building default constructor

Parameterized derived constructor

In the above example, the base class is the default constructor class which is called together with objects from derived/child class. The example below shows base class constructor with parameters.

Syntax

```
class construct

{

        float x;

        public:
```

117

```
    construct(float i)

            {

                    x=i;

        cout << "Parameterized constructor\n";

            }
};


class Child : public construct

{

        float y;

        public:


    Child(float j): construct(j)

            {

        y=j;

                    cout << "Parameterized derived
constructor\n";
```

```
        }


};
```

```
int main()

{

  Child (10);

}
```

```
// output
```

Parameterized constructor

Parameterized derived constructor

An explicit call to the parameterized base constructor class permits a call to the parameterized derived class constructor. A constructor base class is called inside the derived class. This allows the constructor to initialize the object in the class.

A derived class constructor can only access its own class members while a derived class object inherits the characteristics and properties of the base class. A base class constructor initializes the members of the base class.

119

Upcasting in C++

The use of superclass reference or a pointer to point to a subclass object is known as upcasting. That is, converting the subclass reference address or pointer to its superclass reference address.

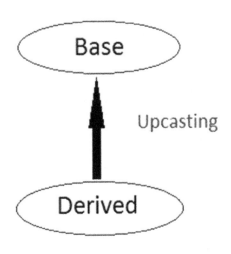

Syntax

class baseclass

{

     int i;

     public:

     void Base()

     {

```
        cout << "This is a Superclass";

        }
};


class derived:public baseclass

{
        int j;

};


int main()

{
        baseclass* ptr;  // pointer to base class

        derived obj;

        ptr = &obj;


        baseclass &ref;  // baseclass's reference address

        ref=obj;

}
```

In a downcasting, the base class's reference or pointer is converted into a derived class reference or its pointer.

Note: Constructors and destructors are not inherited. The assignment operator (=) can be overloaded but it cannot be inherited by a subclass.

Inheritance and Static Functions

1. The static functions can be inherited into the derived class.

2. If static member functions are redefined in a derived class, then other overloaded functions in the super class are hidden.

3. All static member functions cannot be virtual.

Hybrid Inheritance and Virtual Class

When a derived class inherits properties of more than one base class, it results in multiple inheritance. See example below.

Syntax

class BaseA

{

    void print();

```
};


class BaseB:public BaseA

{
        // derived class definition

};


class BaseC:public BaseA

{
        // derived class definition

};


class BaseD:public BaseB, public BaseC

{
        // class definition

};


int main()

{
```

```
    D obj;

    obj.print();

}
```

Class BaseB and BaseC inherit the **print()** function in class BaseA. Class BaseD inherits two copies of the **print()** function. When you call the **print()** in the **main()** function, it results in ambiguity since the compiler doesn't know which **print()** function to call. To avoid this, a virtual function is used. This is done by inserting the virtual keyword when the class is being inherited.

```
class BaseB: virtual public BaseA

{

        // derived class definition

};



class BaseC: virtual public BaseA

{

        // derived class definition

};



class BaseD:public BaseB, public BaseC
```

```
{

    // class definition

};
```

The virtual keyword tells the compiler to call any of the two functions.

Managing Dynamic Data

C++ allows you to dynamically allocate memory space for your program. Initially, a programmer can determine the memory space of the program by defining the variables before the program executes. There are cases where the memory can only be determined during run time or it is based on user input needs. In this case, the memory is dynamically allocated to programs. Dynamic memory determines how the data is processed and stored.

Pointers are also used for memory allocation and hold the memory address of a variable. When you declare a variable it has two components:

- The address of the variable

- The value which is stored in the variable. For example: int y= 200.

The above example tells the compiler to:

1. Create a space in memory to store the value of the variable.

2. Associate the variable *y* with the reserved memory location.

3. Store value 200 at the reserved memory location.

Pointers is one of the useful features in C++ language, and once utilized in a program, it enables:

1. Direct access and manipulation of the memory location.

2. Allocation of dynamic memory into a variable.

3. Improvement of efficiency in some routine programs.

Allocating and Deallocating Memory with New and Delete Operators

C++ program integrates the new and delete operators to dynamically allocate the memory. The **new** operator followed by the data type specifier dynamically allocates the memory of a program.

If the user input has a sequence of more than one element, then the **new[]** operator is need to allocate a block of memory.

Syntax

Pointer = new return-type

or

Pointer = new return-type [size]

The **new** operator allocates memory for a single element on the memory heap.

The **new []** operator allocates memory to an array/block of elements with the size being an integer value that represents the objects returned.

Syntax

```
int *mem;

mem = new int [4];
```

When you run the program, the system dynamically allocates memory space of the 4 elements of integer type and returns an array of elements assigned to pointer mem. Therefore, mem points directly to a memory block with four elements of integer (int) type.

You can access the first element in the array by calling mem [0], while the second element is accessed by mem [1].

You can also initialize the memory with the new operator, as seen below.

Syntax

Pointer-variable= new return-type (value);

Example:

127

```
int *ptr = new int (30);

float *r = new float (15)
```

There exists a difference between a normal array and a block of memory allocated dynamically using the **new** operator. In a normal array, the array size is a **constant** expression which is determined during variable declaration (before running the program), whereas the dynamic memory allocation is performed using the **new** operator that assigns memory space to a program during run time. It uses any variable value as the size for the block of elements.

The system dynamically allocates memory to a program from the memory **heap**. Non-static and local variables are allocated memory on **stack.**

For any dynamically allocated memory **(int *mem= new int[4])** the programmer has to deallocate the memory after the program execution. Otherwise, if the memory space is not deallocated, it will result in a memory leak. The memory should be deallocated after the program execution terminates.

Delete operator

In C++, the operator **delete** deallocates the already allocated memory space to a program. This makes the memory available for the next request to dynamically allocate space.

Syntax

delete pointer-variable;

or

delete [] pointer-variable;

If you dynamically allocated space to a single element using the **new** operator, then use **delete** pointer-variable to free the memory. To free a memory allocated to a block of elements, you use **delete []**. The arguments passed to the delete operator should be either a **pointer** that points to a block of elements or a **null pointer**. Passing a **null pointer** has no effect to the **delete** operator.

For example, delete [] ptr; or delete ptr;

```
#include <iostream>

#include <new>

using namespace std;


int main ()

{

 int l,m;

 int * ptr;

 cout << "Enter the numbers you want to print:";
```

```
cin >> l;

ptr= new (nothrow) int[l];

if (ptr == nullpointer)

        cout << "Error: Unsuccessful memory allocation";

else

{

        for (m=0; m<l; m++)

        {

        cout << "Enter number: ";

        cin >> ptr[m];

        }

        cout << "The numbers entered are: ";

        for (m=0; m<l; m++)

        cout << ptr[m] << ", ";

        delete[] ptr;

}

return 0;

}

// output
```

Enter the numbers you want to print: 3

Enter number: 25

Enter number: 50

Enter number: 72

The numbers entered are: 25, 50, 72

If the system could not allocate the memory space requested for example, requesting a large memory allocation then the system will return an error message. **Error: Unsuccessful memory allocation.** The new request will throw a standard **bad_alloc** exception, unless you use the **nothrow** with the new operator. This exception type handle errors by checking the pointer value or through catching exceptions.

Handling Errors with Try and Catch

Computer memory is a limited resource and sometimes it's not a guarantee whether the request to dynamically allocated memory to a program using the new operator will be successful. The memory gets exhausted sometimes.

C++ uses two standard mechanisms to determine if the memory allocation was successful or not. If memory allocation fails, an exception is thrown. The **nothrow** exception is used to handle the errors in the program instead of throwing **bad_alloc** exception which terminates the program after an error occurred. These will be discussed later in detail.

Syntax

ptr= new (nothrow) int[l];

To know whether the block of memory allocation fails, you can detect the failure through checking whether the pointer variable is null.

Avoiding Memory Leaks

When a programmer creates a memory in the heap and forgets to delete it, it creates a memory leak. To avoid having a memory leak, you should free the memory allocated on the heap when no longer needed. Always make sure to use the right operator (delete or delete []) to deallocate the memory.

If there is a memory leak, then the memory usage increases. This makes the limited memory resource very costly thus creating more problems later. The example below is a program to show a memory leak.

Syntax

#include <iostream.h>

using namespace std;

void memory_leak()

```
{

    int *p = new int(4);


    return; // return method without deallocating the
pointer variable p

}


int main()

{


    // Calling the function

    // function to get the memory leak

    memory_leak();


    return 0;

}
```

Smart pointers can also be used to free the memory. You don't have to manually manage the memory. Instead of declaring **char*** you can use **std::string** which manages the internal memory. This makes it faster and well-optimized compared to when managing memory manually.

You can also reduce memory leaks by reducing the new/delete calls.

Chapter Summary

Inheritance is one of the important features of object oriented programming. It allows programmers to reuse code instead of rewriting the same code again. In this, one class inherits the properties and methods of another class (base class). In this chapter, you have learned:

- How to derive new classes from existing classes so as to promote code reusability.

- How to use inheritance to support overriding methods as well as learn how to work with both base and derived classes.

- How you can specify what properties are to be inherited by the subclass using the access mode. This requires you to define the base class first before defining the subclass.

- About different types of inheritance and how to use each type in creating objects.

- How to use constructors and destructors in deriving objects.

- How to access a class using the base and derived constructors.

134

- How you can call a base class constructor in a derived class constructor. When you create a derived class object from an existing base class, the base class becomes a constructor by default, and it is executed first then followed by the derived class.

- How to make a call of the base class inside the derived class constructor that has parameters like the base class constructor.

- How to use upcasting feature in C++ to allow you to reference your base class.

- How to use a pointer to point directly to a subclass.

- How to dynamically allocate memory space for your program during run-time.

- How to use new and delete operators to allocate and deallocate memory when not needed.

- How to use delete or delete [] operators to help you avoid memory leaks in your program.

- How to use try catch exceptions to test whether memory allocation is successful or has failed.

In the next chapter you will learn about polymorphism. At the end of the chapter you will know what polymorphism is and how to apply different types of polymorphism during compile and runtime. You will also learn how to create abstract classes and virtual functions.

Chapter Five: Polymorphism

Polymorphism is an OOP feature that allows an object to have more than one form. If you have multiple classes that relate to each other by inheritance, the classes are using the polymorphism concept. When using inheritance, polymorphism is executed by use of overriding function. That is, both the superclass and subclass have same declared member function but different function definition.

In our previous chapter, the inheritance feature allowed us to create a new derived class that inherited attributes and properties of another class. Polymorphism uses similar methods to perform different tasks. It allows you to perform a single task using different forms. For example, a woman can have different characteristics depending on the situation, like being a wife, a mother, and an employee.

Polymorphism is divided in two:

- Runtime polymorphism

- Compile time polymorphism

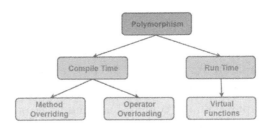

Compile Time Polymorphism

Compile time polymorphism is also known as static polymorphism, and it indicates the existence of an entity in more than one physical form. In static polymorphism, functions are bound based on their signature (data type and the number of parameters present). The function calls represent an early binding because they're made on the basis of data type and the sequence of parameters passed.

Compile time polymorphism is implemented using overriding function and operator overloading.

Overloading Function

Function overloading is a situation where you have multiple functions with the same name but different parameters. These functions have parameters with different data types or changes in the number of parameters being passed.

Syntax

int area (int x);

int area (int x, int y);

See example below.

#include <iostream.h>

using namespace std;

class Addition {

public: float sum(float x, float y){

```cpp
        return x+y;

}

float sum(float x, float y, float z){

        return x+y+z;

 }

};

int main() {

  Addition obj;

  // A call to sum function with two parameters

  cout<<"Total Sum: "<<obj.sum(8.80, 15.20)<<endl;

  //call to the second function with three parameters

  cout<<"Total Sum: "<<obj.sum(18.5, 26.4, 30.0);

  return 0;

}


// output

Total sum: 24.0

Total sum: 74.9
```

Overloading functions improve code readability as well as code reusability as shown above. You can perform the same task to functions with a different parameter list.

Operator Overloading

Operator overloading allows you to overload operators. For example, you can use operator (+) to join two strings together. If you use the addition operator between two integers, it adds them but when the operator is placed between strings, it concatenates or joins them.

To overload an operator, you have to declare a class member function whose name is operator and then follow with the operator sign you want to use.

Type operator-sign (parameters)

For example: xyz operator + (xyz) / using operator overloading

Syntax

```
#include<iostream.h>

using namespace std;

class xyz

{

private:

        int a,b;

public:
```

```
xyz()

void getvalues()

{

cout<<"Enter value of a and b";

cin>>a>>b;

}

void setvalues(float x, float y)

{

x=a;

y=b;

}

void setvalues(double num1, double num2)

{

num1=a;

    num2=b;

}

void display()

{

    cout<<"The value for a is:"<<a<<"The value for b
is:"<<b<<endl;

    }
```

```
        Double addition()

        xyz operator + (xyz)


};

xyz xyz::operator +(xyz)

{

        return (a+b)

}

int main()

{

        xyz x1,x2,x3;

        x1.getvalues(10,15);

        x2.setvalues(6,8);

        x3.setvalues(12,8);

        cout<<x1.addition();

        cout<<x2.addition();

        cout<<x3.addition();

        return 0;

}
```

Run-time Polymorphism

Run time polymorphism is also dynamic polymorphism. In this type of polymorphism, functions change their form depending on the situation. If a function exists in different forms and responds to different function calls made dynamically during running time, then it forms dynamic polymorphisms.

Runtime polymorphism supports dynamic binding and makes programs more flexible when being executed.

In dynamic binding, a function call is made at run-time and it depends on the function pointer content at run-time. If you change the contents of the function pointer, you will end up with different functions that share the same name but have different function body.

A dynamic polymorphism changes an entity based on the situation. A function exhibits dynamic polymorphism if it exists in different forms. The function calls to these types of polymorphism are made dynamically during the execution time.

Dynamic binding is also known as late binding, and it improves the flexibility of a program being executed. The calls to the function are made on the basis of content of function pointer. All polymorphic functions have the same name but with different data types or sequence of parameters.

Static binding is more efficient than dynamic binding in some cases. If you have a static function you don't need a run-time search, while dynamic functions calls for run-time search. Most function calls in dynamic binding are resolved at execution time.

Dynamic polymorphism is implemented using overriding functions and virtual functions.

Overriding Function

Function overriding allows you to have the same function name in the superclass and subclass. The subclass inherits the data members and member functions in the superclass. You can create an overriding function in the subclass by creating the same member functions with the same argument list.

Function overriding is done only in the derived class, and it is achieved during run time. Overriding function is redefining a base class inside the derived class with the same return type and parameters.

Syntax

```
class Super
{
        public:
   void print()
        {
        cout << "This is a base class";
        }
```

143

```
};


class Subclass: public Super

{

        public:

        void print()

        {

        cout << "This is a Derived Class";

        }
};
```

The print () in the base class is overridden in the derived class.

How to call overriding function

You can make a call to the overriding function in the **main ()** function. The function call and the function body connects through the binding process. If the connections occur before run time it is called early binding, static or compile-time binding.

Syntax

```
class Super

{
```

```cpp
    public:
  void print()
        {
        cout << "This is a base class";
        }
};


class Subclass: public Super
{
        public:
        void print()
        {
        cout << "This is a Derived Class";
        }
};
int main ()
{
    Super b; //creating object for base class
    Subclass d; // creating object for derived class
```

145

```
b.print(); // static binding

d.print();

return 0;

}
```

//output

This is a base class

This is a derived class

See below for an example of calling the above base function using pointers.

```
int main ()

{

Super *b; //creating object pointer for base class

Subclass d; // creating object for derived class

b = &d;

b -> print (); // static binding

}
```

In the above example, we have made a call to the overridden function using base object and derived object. The **b.print ()** object will call the base function while **d.print ()** object will call the derived class function.

146

Virtual Functions

A virtual function is a base class member function which is overridden in the derived class. The function call results in **late binding.** That is, it instructs the compiler to perform late binding on the overridden function.

To make member functions of the base class virtual, a **virtual** keyword is used when declaring the function. A late binding call is made at run time. Therefore, the compiler determines the object type during run time and makes the function call.

Virtual void function-name()

{//function body}

Example:

```
#include <iostream.h>


  class car

  {

  public:

    virtual void make()

    {

      cout<<"member function of the car base class is accessed";
```

```
    }

};

class 4wheel: public car

{

public:

    void make()

    {

        cout<<"Accessing virtual member function of the
4wheel derived class";

    }

};


    void main()

    {

        car *a, *b;

        a = new car();

        a -> make(); //an object pointer which is equivalent to
*a.make();

        b = new car();

        b -> make();
```

}

If a member of the class is redefined inside the derived class, it is called a virtual member. In the above example, function **make()** is a virtual function inside the base class. A 4wheeler is a derived class of the base class car.

If the member function is not declared as virtual then it will result in static binding where the function call is bound during compile time. But if the function is declared as virtual, the function address is bound during run-time making it a dynamic binding.

To achieve dynamic binding concept, the compiler creates a **v-table** every time a virtual function is declared. The v-table contains information about the function pointers from each of the objects in the derived class and other function class information. This information is made available whenever a call is made to the virtual function.

How to Access Private Member Functions in a Derived Class Using Virtual Keyword

Using virtual keyword, you can easily call the private member function in a derived class with a pointer that points to the base class. In this case, the compiler will look at the access specifier mode during compile time.

During late binding when the program is running, the compiler doesn't check the access specifier of the function being called.

Syntax

```cpp
class Super

{

        public:

   virtual void print()

        {

        cout << "This is a base class";

        }

};


class Subclass: public Super

{

        public:

        virtual void print()

        {

        cout << "This is a Derived Class";

        }

};

int main ()

        {
```

```
Super *b;

Subclass d;

b = &d;

b -> print ();

}
```

// output

This is a derived class

Notes:

1. Only the base class function is declared with a virtual keyword.

2. If you declare a function as virtual in the base class, then the function will automatically be virtual in all of the derived classes.

Abstract Classes

An abstract class is a type of class which consists of at least a pure virtual function. Abstract class provides an interface to a derived class. If a class inherits properties of an abstract class, then you must define the pure virtual function, otherwise, the derived class will become an abstract class.

Characteristics of abstract class:

1. Even though you can create pointers and references in an abstract class, it cannot be instantiated.

2. Abstract class has both variables, functions and a pure virtual function.

3. Abstract classes are suitable in performing upcasting so as to allow the subclass to use its interface.

4. All classes that inherit the properties of an abstract class must implement the pure virtual function, to avoid becoming abstract too.

Pure Virtual Function

A virtual function with no definition is known as the pure virtual function. A pure virtual function has no function body and it uses the **virtual** keyword at the beginning and ends with a notation **=0** since it has no body.

Virtual void function-name () =0;

Both virtual and pure functions works the same way except that the pure virtual function has no function definition.

The example below demonstrates an abstract class.

class BPolygon

```
{
protected:
        float width, height;
public:
        void setvalues(float x, float y)
        {
        width=x; height=y;
        }
        virtual float area()=0;
};
class BRectangle:public BPolygon
{
public:
        float area()
        {
        return (width*height);
        }
};
class BTriangle:public BPolygon
```

153

```cpp
{
public:

        float area()

        {

        return ((width*height)/2);

        }

};

int main()

{

        BRectangle rect;

        BTriangle tri;

        BPolygon *p1=&rect;

        BPolygon *p2=&tri;

        p1 -> setvalues(8,6);

        *p2.setvalues(8,6);

        cout<<p1 ->area()<<endl;

        cout<<p2 ->area()<<endl;

        return 0;

}
```

Chapter Summary

In this chapter you have learned what polymorphism is and the different types of polymorphisms. You're now able to:

- Differentiate between the compile time polymorphism and run time polymorphism using examples.

- Use static binding or early binding to make system calls to the member function and how to use dynamic binding to make a function call during program execution.

- Use function overloading and operator overloading to increase program efficiency.

- Make function calls using overriding functions and virtual functions as well as override a function inside a derived class.

- Declare virtual functions in your program and know how to use abstract classes.

- Access the private member functions using the virtual keyword as well as differentiate between a virtual function and a pure virtual function.

In the next chapter you will learn about constructors and destructors. By the end of the chapter, you will be able to declare class constructor and destructor and know how to use different types of constructors.

Chapter Six: Constructors and Destructors

Overview

A **constructor** is a member function which initializes the objects of a class type and has the same name as the class name. The constructor class can accept arguments or not accept arguments, and it allocates memory space to class objects.

Constructor's member function performs construction work. That is, building values in an object through automatic initialization. A constructor is automatically invoked whenever a new instance of a class is created. You can define the arguments of the class manually or leave it without any arguments.

The name of the constructor is always the same as the name of the class and the constructor has no return type.

Class ConstructorName

{// class body};

On the other hand, a **destructor** is a member function that is complementary to the constructor. A destructor de-initializes an object after it has been destroyed. The destructor function call is made when an object within a class has gone out of scope, or when its memory space is de-allocated with the use of **delete** operator.

The destructor de-allocates memory space for the object. A destructor doesn't have any parameters, therefore it cannot be overloaded. It is usually called in reverse to constructor. If a class (derived class) inherits properties of another class (base class) and both classes have destructor, then the destructor in the derived class is called first.

A destructor has the same name as the class and the tilde (~) operator precedes it.

~ Class Name

{// class body};

Definition and Declaration of a Constructor

A constructor definition is just like the other member functions in a class. The definition is either inside the class or outside the class using the class name followed by the scope resolution :: operator.

Syntax

Class Base

{

        double a, b;

        Protected:

        Base (double, double); // constructor

        Void print ()

};

The class base has a member function constructor **Base ()** which has the same name as the class Base. This member function is the constructor of the class and it can be utilized in order to create values for the object class. When making a call to the function, you can pass values to the function by declaring the object.

Base b; // object declaration

B= Base (35, 58);

In this case, an object b is created from the Base class and a constructor call is prompted.

See below for an example of a constructor demonstration.

```
#include <iostream>

#include <conio.h>

Class Triangle

{

private:

        double length, height;

public:

        length = 15.2;

        height = 20.5;
```

```
double area()

{

return (length*height/2);

}


};

int main()

{

        clrscr();

        Triangle tri;

        cout<<"The area of triangle is:"
<<tri.area()<<"sq.units\n";

        getch();

}
```

// output

The area of triangle is: 155.8 sq.units

Characteristics of Constructors

1. They should always be declared under the public access specifier.

2. Constructors don't have a return type, not even a null (void) return type.

3. Creating a new object results in an automatic call to the constructor function.

4. A derived class can't inherit a constructor function but it can make a call to the base class constructor.

5. A constructor can have default parameters just like other functions.

6. Constructors can never work as virtual functions.

7. You can't refer to the address of a constructor.

Types of Constructors

C++ programming language has various types of constructors which extend its functionality. These constructors include: default, parameterized, overloaded and copy.

Default constructors

A default constructor doesn't have any arguments or parameters. See example below.

Class Cube

{

Public:

```
        int x;

        Cube()

        {

        X= 5;

        }

};
int main ()

  {

        Cube c;

        Cout<< c.x;

  }
```

Once the object is created, a call to the constructor is made immediately, thus initializing the data member. The default constructor initializes the object members. If you don't define a constructor, the compiler implicitly assigns a default constructor to the class.

If a compiler returns a default constructor, it will initialize the object data members with a default value which is initially 0 or any random integer value.

Parameterized constructors

This is a constructor which has arguments. You can supply different parameters or values to the data members of different objects.

The initial values to the constructor are passed as arguments when the constructor is declared. This is done by:

- Calling the constructor explicitly.

- Calling the constructor implicitly.

See example below.

```
Class Cube

{

  Public:

        int val;

        Cube( int x)

        {

        val= x;

        }

};

int main ()

  {
```

162

```
Cube c (5);

Cube c1 (10);

Cube c2 (15);

cout<< c.val;

cout<< c1.val;

cout<< c2.val;

}
```

Overloaded constructor

Constructors not only initialize data members, they're not different from other member functions. They also perform function overloading just like in polymorphism. The default and parameterized constructors can act as an overloaded constructor where one of them has no parameters while the other one has parameters.

Overloaded constructor allows you to have multiple constructors in a class with each having different parameter list.

See example below.

```
#include <iostream>

using namespace std;

class overload
```

```cpp
{
public:

    double area;

    overload()
    {
    area = 0;
    }

    overload(float num1, float num2)
    {
    area = num1 * num2;
    }

    void display()
    {
    cout<< area<< endl;
    }
};
int main()
{
```

// constructor overloading with same class name and different arguments

overload c1;

overload c2(8.6, 6.2);

c1.display();

c2.display();

}

// output

0

53.32

Copy constructors

C++ offers a special type of constructor which passes an object as a parameter to the function and copy data member values from one object to another. Copy constructor declares and initializes object values from another object.

Copy constructor creates new objects with exact features as the existing object, hence the name copy constructor. A copy constructor acts as overloaded constructor because it declares and initializes an object from another object.

165

There are two types of copy constructors:

- Default copy constructor: The compiler automatically defines this type of copy constructor if the user or programmer doesn't define the copy constructor.

- User defined constructor: It is a copy constructor defined by the programmer.

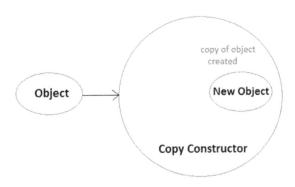

Syntax

Class_name (const class_name & object_name);

Example 1:

Class Copy

{

    Copy (Copy &y) // copy constructor

```
{ // function body of copy constructor }
```

```
};
```

To call the copy constructor in the above example, you have to initialize the object. This can be done in any of the following ways:

```
Copy c2 (c1);
```

or

```
Copy c2=c1
```

Where,

c1 initializes the c2 object.

Example 2:

```
#include <iostream>

using namespace std;

class Copy

{

public:

float i;

Copy(float x) //parameterized constructor.

{
```

```
    i=x;

}

Copy(Copy &y)  // copy constructor definition

{

i = y.i;

}

};

int main()

{

Copy c1(35);  // Call to parameterized constructor.

Copy c2(c1);   //  Call to copy constructor.

cout<<c2.i;

return 0;

}
```

// output

35

When a call is made to the constructor, two copies are produced:

- Shallow copy

- Deep copy

Shallow copy

The default copy constructor created by the compiler can only produce a shallow copy. It is a shallow copy since the objects are created by copying all data variables of an object to another object.

See the example below:

```
class Example
{
        int num1;

        int num2;

        int *ptr;

        public:

        Example()

        {

        ptr=new int;

        }

        void setdata(int a,int b,int c)

        {
```

```cpp
        num1=a;

        num2=b;

        *ptr=c;

        }

        void printdata()

        {

        std::cout << "Num1 value is : " <<num1<<
std::endl;

        std::cout << "Num2 value is : " <<num2<<
std::endl;

        std::cout << "*ptr value is : " <<*ptr<< std::endl;

        }

};

int main()

{

 Example e1;

 e1.setdata (8, 9, 12);

 Example e2 = e1;

 e2.printdata();

        return 0;
```

```
}
```

// output

Num1 value is: 8

Num2 value is: 9

*ptr value is: 12

In the above example, the constructor is not defined, therefore the compiler assigns example **e2**= **e1** by calling the default copy constructor. In this case, the compiler creates a similar copy of the existing object. The pointer **ptr** points to the same memory location on both objects.

If the memory of one of the objects is freed, the other memory is automatically freed since both fields point to the same memory. To avoid this problem, you can define the copy constructor (user-defined constructor) that uses deep copy technique.

Deep copy

Deep copy is a technique where memory is dynamically allocated to a copy and then it copies the actual values. The source and the copy have distinct characteristics and won't share the same memory location.

In deep copy, the programmer has to write a user-defined constructor.

171

Syntax

```
class Example
{
        Public:
        int num1;
        int num2;
        int *ptr;
        Example()
        {
        ptr=new int;
        }
        Example (Example &y)
        {
        num1=y.num1;
        num2=y.num2;
        ptr=new int;
        *ptr=*(y.ptr);
        }
        void setdata(int a,int b,int c)
        {
        num1=a;
```

172

```
        num2=b;

        *ptr=c;

        }

        void printdata()

        {

        std::cout << "Num1 value is : " <<num1<< std::endl;

        std::cout << "Num2 value is : " <<num2<< std::endl;

        std::cout << "*ptr value is : " <<*ptr<< std::endl;

        }

};

int main()

{

 Example e1;

 e1.setdata (5, 7, 9);

 Example e2 = e1;

 e2.printdata();

        return 0;

}

// output
```

Num1 value is: 5

Num2 value is: 7

*ptr value is: 9

Since the programmer defined the constructor, then **e2=e1** calls for an already user-defined copy constructor. This result to an exact copy of the object which is pointed by ***ptr** and all the values on the type data members.

Class Destructor

A destructor has a special member function which executes when the delete operation is invoked in the object of that class or when an object in the class gets out of scope.

A destructor will have the same name as the class with a prefix of the tilde operator. It has no return values, and you can't pass any parameters to it. Destructor is an important C++ feature which frees memory space when it's no longer needed.

Example: The following example explains how to use constructors and destructors in a program.

Syntax

```
// constructor & destructor

Class CRectangle

{
```

```
int *len, *wid;

public:

        CRectangle (int, int)// constructor

        ~CRectangle ()//destructor

        int area()

        {

        return (len*wid);

        }

};

CRectangle:: CRectangle (int c, int d)

{

        *len=c;

        *wid=d;

};

//destructor to free the memory

CRectangle :: CRectangle ()

{

        delete len;

        delete wid;
```

```
};

int main()

{

        CRectangle.rect a (c,d);

        CRectangle.rect b (c,d);

        cout << Area of a rectangle is: <<rect a.area();

        cout << Area of a rectangle is: <<rect b.area();

        cout << endl;


}
```

Special Characteristics of Destructors

1. When an object is destroyed, a constructor is called automatic.

2. Just like other member functions, destructors follow the same access rules.

3. A destructor de-initializes an object before it gets out of scope.

4. Destructors don't have a return type and do not even support void.

5. Destructor functions can never be inherited.

6. A destructor doesn't allow the use of static destructors.

7. A destructor can make calls to member functions of it's class.

8. If an object in a class has a destructor, then that object can't be a member of the union.

Chapter Summary

In this chapter, you have learned about constructor, destructor and functions overload. Constructors are very essential in C++ language since they help build values in objects through automatic initialization. Specifically, you learned:

- How to declare and initialize constructors.

- How a constructor initializes an object of the class type.

- How a destructor de-initializes the object after execution. A destructor helps free the memory space by de-initializing the object after it has been destroyed.

- About parameterized constructors with parameters. You will be able to pass different parameters and values to the data members on different objects. You also learned how to make calls to the constructor.

- How to use the overloaded constructor and copy constructor.

- To understand the two types of copy constructors: shallow and deep.

- How to create a project with both types of copy constructors and how to make calls to the objects created.

In the next chapter you will learn how to use templates. At the end of the chapter you will be able to create class templates, function temples and how to create templates with multiple parameters.

Chapter Seven:
Templates

Introduction to Templates

Templates are an important feature in C++ programming language, as it allows functions and classes to use generic types. They play an essential role on how functions and classes work by allowing them to define different data types without rewriting each other.

Using templates, you can write a generic code that can be used with any data type. All you need is to pass the data types as parameters. Templates promote code reusability and improve the flexibility of the program. You can create a simple class or a function and pass data types as parameters and implement the code to be used by any data type. Whenever you want to use the function, you make a call to the function and specify the return type.

For example, if you use **sort()** function to sort data in a warehouse, you can pass different data types as parameters to the function. You don't have to write and maintain multiple file codes to sort data. Based on the data type passed to the sorting algorithm, your data in the warehouse is sorted irrespective of that particular data type. Therefore, templates are used in situations where you need a code to be reusable with more than one data type.

Templates are of great importance when dealing with multiple inheritance and operator overloading. It is widely applied where code reusability is of prime importance.

179

Types of Templates

Templates are implemented in two ways:

- Using function templates

- Using class templates

A template can be defined as a macro. That is, when you define an object of a specific type, the template definition of that type of class substitutes it with the appropriate data type. Templates are often referred to as parameterized class or functions since a specified data type will replace the defined parameter during execution time.

Class Templates

Class templates offer the specifications for creating a class based on the parameters. A class template accepts members with parameter type. That is, you can instantiate a class template by passing a given set of data type to its parameter list. Class templates are mostly used in implementing containers.

Syntax

Template <class identifier>

Class class-name

{

...

//class member specifications

...

};

Example:

```
Template <class M>
Class vector
{
  M*v;  //type M vector
  int size, sum;

  public:
    vector(int n )
    {
      v=new M [size = n];
      for(int j=0; j<size; j++) v[j] =0;
    }

    vector (M* a)
    {
      for(int j=0;j<size; j++)
      v[j]=a[j];
    }

    M operator*( vector &y)
    {
      M sum =0;
      for(int j=0;j<size;j++)
      sum+= -> v[j]*y-v[j];
      return sum;
    }
};
```

A class template definition is similar to normal class definition except that in templates, you add a prefix template **<class M>** where, M is the type. The template prefix tells the compiler that a class template is declared which uses M as the type name in the declaration. In this case, the class vector is a parameterized class that uses type M as its arguments. Type M can be replaced by any data type or by using a user-defined data type.

If a class is derived from a class template, then it's called a **template class**. The objects of the template class are defined as follows:

Classname<type> objectname (arglist);

Creating a derived class from class template is known as **instantiation process.** Before creating a template class, you have to debug the class template before converting it to a template class. The compiler checks for errors in a template class after instantiation has taken place.

Example: class template

```
template <Class TT>

Class Rectangle

{

  TT width;

  TT height;

public:

  void setvalues(TT num1,TT num2)

  TT area()

  {

    TT A;

    A=width*height;
```

```
        return A;

    }

};

void Rectangle <TT> ::setvalues (TT num1,TT num2)

{

    width=num1;

    height=num2;

}

int main()

{

    Rectangle obj1;

    Rectangle <int> obj1(5,6);

    Rectangle obj2;

    Rectangle <float> obj2(5.6,4);

    cout<< obj1.setvalues()

    cout<<obj2.setvalues()

    return 0;

}
```

//output

obj1=30

obj2=22.4

The above program creates a class of type TT. The <TT> in the (void Rectangle <TT> ::setvalues (TT num1,TT num2)) statement specifies that the function parameter is also a class template parameter and should always be included when calling a class.

Class Templates with Multiple Parameters

You can also have more than one generic data type in a class. You can declare the generic type class with a comma-separated list inside the template specification.

Syntax

Template <Class xy, Class xyz, ...>

Class class-name

{

   //function body;

};

Example: class with two generic types

```
template<class f1,class f2>

class numbers

{

    f1 j; f2 k;

public:

    numbers (f1 x, f2 y)

    { j=x; k=y;

    }

    void print()

    {

        cout<<j<<"and"<<k<<"\n";

    }

};

int main()

{

Numbers <float, int> numbers1 (2.53, 253);

Numbers <int, char> numbers2 (50,'Z');

numbers1.print();
```

```
numbers2.print();

return 0;

};

// output
```

1.53 and 253

50 and Z

Function Templates

Function templates work like a normal function except that the normal function works with only a single data type, while templates accommodate multiple data types. With templates, you can overload a normal function so as to work with different data types.

This makes function templates more useful since you only have to write a single program that works on all data types.

Templates are always expanded during compile time.

Just like class template, you can create a function template with different argument types.

Syntax

Template <class type>

Return-type function-name (arguments)

{

Function body;

};

When defining function templates, you must include the template type in both the function body and parameter list when necessary.

Example1: Function to swap values

Template <Class T1>

Void swap (T1&num1, T1&num2)

{T1 val= num1; num1=num2; num2=val;};

Calling a template function works the same way as the normal function call.

Example 2: Implementation of function template

template <class test>

test max (test x, test y);

{

    test results;

    results=x>y? x:y;

    return results;

};

int main()

```
{

    int a=5, b=6, c;

    double l=4, m=6, n;

    c= max <int> (a,b);

    n=max <double> (l,m);

    cout<< c<<endl;

    cout<<n<<endl;

    return 0;

}
```

In this example, test is the template parameter. The function max is called twice with different argument types (int and double). When the compiler instantiates, it calls the function each time by its type.

The output object produced (after instantiation of the template with specific type) will be of the same type with the parameters x and y.

The above program will sort values based on which is higher. If using an array of numbers, the sorting algorithm will be applied to sort the numbers from the smallest to highest.

Function Template with Multiple Parameters

Just like in class templates, you can have more than one generic data type separated by commas.

188

```
template<class T1 , class T2, .....>
returntype functionname(arguments of types T1, T2, ...)
{
......
......
......
}
```

Example: Temple class with multiple parameters

```
template<class Temp1,class Temp2>

void display( Temp1 j, Temp2 k)

{

cout<<j<<" "<<k<<"\n";

}

int main()

{

j=display1(2019, "EDGE");

K=display2(18.54, "1854);

 return 0;

}
```

// output

2019   EDGE

18.54   1854

Overloading Template Functions

You can overload a template function using its template function or using the ordinary function from its name. Overloading can be done through:

1. Calling an ordinary function that matches the template function.

2. Calling a template function which is built with the exact function.

3. Use normal overloading function on an ordinary function and make a function call to the one that matches the template function.

If there is no match found, an error message is generated by the system.

Example: Overloaded template using an explicit function

```
template <class M>

 void display(M n)

{

cout<<"Display template function:" << n<< "\n";

}

void display ( int n)

{
```

```
cout<<"Explicit template display: "<< n<<"\n";

}

int main()

{

  display (80);   display (15.20);

  return 0;

}
```

//output

Explicit template display: 80 Display template function: 15.20

The function call **display (80)** calls the ordinary version of a **display ()** function and not its template version.

Member Function Templates

When creating class templates, all member functions can be defined outside the class since the member functions in a template class are parameterized using type argument. Therefore, the function template should define the member functions.

Member functions (whether inline or non-inline) declared inside a class template are implicitly a function

191

template. If a template class is declared, it inherits all the template functions defined in a class template.

Member function templates are defined in three ways:

1. Explicit definition in a file scope for each return-type used to instantiate a template class.

2. During file scope within the template parameters.

3. Inclined within the class.

A member function template can instantiate functions not explicitly generated. If a class has both a member function and an explicit function, then the explicit definition is given more priority.

Syntax

```
Template <class T>
returntype classname <T> :: functionname(arglist)
{
......
.........
........
}
```

Example: Class vector with member function template

```
template<class T>
class vector
{ T*v;
int size; public: vector(int m); vector(T* a);
T operator*(vector & y);
};
//member function templates template<class T>
vector<T> :: vector (int m );
{
v=new T[size=m]; for(int i=0; i<size ; i++) v[i]= 0;
}

template<class T>
vector <T>::vector(t*a)
{
for(int i=0; i<size ; i++)
v[i]=a[i];
}
template< class T >
T vector < T > :: operator*(vector & y)
{
T sum =0;
for ( int i=0; i< size ; i++)
sum += this -> v[i]*y.v[i];
return sum;
}
```

Non-type Template Arguments

Templates can have single or multiple type arguments. You can also use a non-type argument template in addition to the type T argument. You can create a template argument using strings, constants, built-in types and function names.

```
Template<class T, int size> Class array
{
T a[size];                    //automatic array initialization
//............
//...........
};
```

The above template passes the size of an array as an argument. The compiler will only know the size of the

193

array during the execution time. The arguments are specified during the creation of template class.

Chapter Summary

C++ programming language supports the use of templates concept in order to support generic programming. In this chapter, we are able to learn how templates allow us to create a family of classes or functions which can handle different data types. Other functions of templates you have learned include:

- Use of templates to avoid duplication of codes by just making a call to the template function argument return-type. This also makes it easy to manage the program as well as make the program development process easier.

- Creating templates by use of multiple parameters for both class templates and function templates.

- How to create a derived class from a class template which is called a template class. The process used in the creation of the template class is known as instantiation.

- Template functions and how you can overload the template function by either calling the ordinary function that matches the template name or by calling the template function which has an exact match to the function template.

- How to use arguments in class templates. All member functions of the class should be defined as a function template by using the arguments in a class template.

- How to instantiate member functions which are explicitly generated.

- How to use non-type arguments to define and declare function templates.

In the next chapter you will learn about the input and output streams and various file operation methods. At the end of the chapter, you will be able to use ios formatting functions, manage output with manipulators, design your own manipulators, carry out file operations, determine end of file, file opening modes, use put (), get () functions and using file stream classes.

Chapter Eight:
C++ Input and Output Streams

Introduction

C++ programming language comes with a lot of libraries which helps in performing input output functions. The input output concept is performed through a series of bytes which are commonly known as streams. It supports two types of input/output streams with one stream inherited from the C programming language and the other from the object oriented input/output system. Just like the I/O streams in the C programming language, the I/O system in C++ language are fully integrated.

Every developed program takes in data as input, the data is processed then displayed out as an output. This is based on the input output processing cycle or fetch and execute cycle. C++ supports all the I/O function found in C language. The I/O methods in C++ supports object oriented programming concept and user defined data types.

Implementation of I/O operations in C++ is by use of streams concept and stream classes are achieved through the console and disk files.

Both input stream and output streams are used in class definition.

C++ Streams

A stream acts as a logical device which accepts input data and generates information. It is linked to a physical device via the I/O system. Even though the devices connected to the streams work the same, the devices may differ from one another.

Since streams behave in the same manner, their I/O functions can operate in any device. For example, you can use the same function to write to a file, printer, scanner, and display unit.

The stream is both the source and the destination. The source stream supplies data to the program and is commonly known as the **input stream.** On the other hand, a destination stream receives information as output and it is called an **output stream.**

Input stream: This involves flow of bytes from an input device like keyword into the main memory for processing.

Output stream: This is the flow of bytes or processed data from the main memory into an output device like the display screen.

C++ has both **cin** and **cout** as the predefined streams in its standard library. These streams are automatically triggered when a program begins to execute. **Cin** stream is an input stream that is connected to the standard input device and allows the user to enter new data into the system memory, while the **cout** represents the output stream which is connected to an output device to display information.

C++ Stream Classes

I/O system in C++ consists of a hierarchy of classes which define streams for handling the system console unit and disk files. Stream class hierarchy performs both input and output operations within the console unit. The I/O stream classes are declared in the header file of iostream. The header file should be inserted in every program that communicates with the console.

The ios acts as the base class for input stream (**istream**) and **ostream** (output stream) acts as the base class for **iostream** (input/output stream). The **ios class** is declared as a virtual base class and as a result, only a single copy of its data members will be inherited by the **iostream** (input/output stream.)

The ios class offers basic support for I/O operations on both formatted and unformatted streams. It supports handling of both input and output stream. The istream class is responsible for formatted and unformatted input while the ostream class is responsible for formatted output through inheritance concept.

Console Operation Using Stream Classes

Class Name	Properties
ios (basic input/output stream)	Has basic properties that can be used by other input and output classes. Has pointers for buffering objects. Declare functions and constants essential for performing formatted input and output operations.
istream (input stream)	It inherits ios properties. Used to declare get (), getline(), and read () input functions. Consists of overloaded extraction operator >>
ostream (output stream)	It inherits ios properties. Allows you to declare output functions like put() and write(). Uses overloaded insertion operator <<
iostream (input/output stream)	Inherits all characteristics of ios stream and ostream through the use of multiple inheritance. It has both input and output functions of both classes.
streambuf	Provides interface to all physical devices via the buffer. It works as the base class of filebuf available in ios files.

Unformatted Input/Output Operations

Overloaded Operators >> and <<

C++ **cin** and **cout** standard library functions for input and output uses overloaded operators >> and << respectively. The >> operator is overloaded in the istream class while << operator is overloaded in the ostream class.

To read input data from the keyword, you use the >> operator.

cin>> variable 1....>>variable n;

The input variable 1 up to variable n is a variable name which has already been declared inside the class. The cin standard tells the computer to search for the input data from the input devices like keyboard.

The data is read character by character and assigned to the indicated location by the >> operator. Data inputs are separated by white spaces and if the compiler encounters the white spaces when reading a variable or encounters a character that doesn't match the destination data type, it terminates.

Suppose you have a class with a variable declared as an integer, you can use the input data device to input the data.

int num;

cin>> num;

The **cin** statement followed by >> operator will prompt you to enter any value of integer type from the keyboard like 520. When you enter the input data, the operator reads the value 520 assigned to the num variable.

To display the data on the screen, you use the **cout** statement.

cout<< data1<< data 2.... <<data n;

The data1 all the way to data n can be a variable or a constant of any data type.

Put () and Get () Functions

The istream and ostream classes defines two types of member functions **get()**, and **put()** to handle input/ output operations of a single character.

The **get()** functions is represented into two forms of function prototype. That is, the **get(char*)** and the **get(void)**. These function prototypes fetch a new character, a blank space, newline and even a tab in the input data. The **get(char*)** prototype assigns input character to the function arguments while **get(void)** only returns the input character.

The function prototypes represent member functions of input/output stream and they should be invoked using an appropriate object.

201

Example:

Char i;

cin.get(i) // this allows you to get a character from the keyboard and assign to variable i.

{

Cout<<i // display the variable on the screen

}

The above code reads and displays a line of text statements. The >> operator in the cout statement reads a character by character and skips any white spaces or new line character in the statement.

cin>>i; can be used instead of cin.get(i)

Where,

i=cin.get();

In this, the value of the member function **get()** is assigned to the variable i.

Put() is a member function of ostream class and it outputs a single line of statements or a character by character. For example:

cout.put(i);

This code displays a single character **i** while **cout.put(ch)** displays the value to the **ch** variable. You pass any number variable as argument to the **put()** member function.

Example:

```
char x; cin.get (x); while(x!=\n)
{
    cout.put(x);

    cin.get(x);
}
```

A program using get() and put () to represent I/O data.

```
# include<iostream>
using namespace std;


int main()
{
        int m=0;

        char n;

        cout<<"enter input text"

        cin.get(n);
```

```
    while (n1=\n)

    {

        cout.put(n);

        m++;cin.get(n);

    }



    cout<<\n Number of characters="<m<< "\n";

    return 0;

}
```

Input

C++ programming language.

Output

C++ programming language.

Number of characters = 22

Getline() and Write() Function

The **getline()** and **write()** functions are responsible for reading or displaying a line of text in an effective manner. The **getline()** reads a whole line of text which has a new line character "**\n**". When the compiler encounters the new line character, the program is executed. A call to the function is made through:

cin.getline (line, size);

The function call invokes getline() function which reads the characters entered to the system via the keyboard. Once the **size-1** or **\n** character is encountered, the reading is terminated.

Example:

char EmpName [30];

cin.getline(EmpName, 30);

Example:

```
#include <iostream>

using namespace std;

int main()
{
        int size=30;

        char country[30];

        cout<<"enter the name of the country:\n ";

        cin>>country;

        cout<<"country    name    is:"<<country<<"\n\n";
cout<<"enter another country name again: \n";

        cin.getline(country,size);
```

```
        cout<<"The        current        country        name
is:"<<country<<"\n\n";

        return 0;

}
```

//output

enter the name of the country: Kenya

enter another country name again: Uganda

the current country name is: Uganda

The write() function display the whole line and uses the following form:

cout.write(line, size)

The line argument indicates the string's name displayed and the size argument shows the number of characters. If the variable size is greater than the program line, then beyond the bound of the line is displayed.

Formatted Console I/O Operations

There are various features supported by C++ to help format the output. These features include:

- ios class function and flags.

- User-defined output functions.

- Manipulators.

ios Format Functions

The ios class has a large number of functions for formatting the output in a number of ways. These member functions include:

Member Function	Manipulators	Action
Width()	Setw()	This function indicates the required field size needed to display an output value.
fill()	Setfill()	It specifies the characters essential for filling unused portion of the field.
Precision()	Setprecision()	Indicates the number of digits which are to be displayed after the decimal point of float value.
Setf()	Setioflags()	It specifies the format flag used to control what form of output is to be displayed.
Unsetf()	Resetiosflags()	It clears any specified flag

When included in the I/O statements, these manipulators change the parameter format of a stream. To access manipulator functions in a program, you have to include **iomanip** file.

Defining Field Width

The **width()** function determines the width field needed for the output of an object. You can invoke the function through:

cout.width(w);

Where,

w is the width field and it is printed in a field of w characters wide. The function specifies the field width for a single object. After printing the output details of the single object, it reverts back to default settings.

For example, cout.width(7);

cout<<6543<<12<<"\n"; // printing in the format of 6, 5, 4, 3 and 1, 2

This will produce the following output:

	6	5	4	3	1	2

Setting Precision (Precision ())

When working with floating point numbers, they're printed six digits after the decimal point. To avoid printing

208

all these six digits, you can specify the number of digits to be printed after the decimal point. This can easily be achieved by the use of **precision ()** member function.

cout.precision (d);

Where,

d is the number of digits after the decimal point are to be printed. The function retains its setting until they're reset, unlike the width ().

Example:

cout.precision (3)

Filling and Padding

The unused part of field width is always filled up with white spaces. The **fill()** function is used to fill these unused white spaces with any desired character.

Cout.fill (ch);

Where,

ch is the character used in filling up the unused white spaces.

Example:

Count.fill ('*')

In this case, the white spaces will be filled with '*' operator. For example, some institutions like banks use this form of filling blank spaces, especially when printing a cheque.

Formatting Flags, Bit fields and Setf()

The **setf ()** is ios class member function for justifying answers.

cout.setf (arg1, arg2)

Where,

arg 1 is the already formatting flag in ios class. The flag indicates the formatting requirements of an output. Arg2 is an ios constant which specifies the formatting group to which the formatting flag belongs to.

Example:

cout.setf (ios::left, ios::adjustfield);

cout.setf (ios::scientific, ios::floatfield);

The first statement in the above example should have a group member to the second statement.

Example:

cout.fill (*);

cout.setf (ios::left, ios::adjustified);

cout.width (8);

cout<<"flag"<<"\n";

// output

F	L	A	G		*	*	*

Using Manipulator to Manage Output

The **iomanip** header file has a set of manipulator functions which manipulates the output format. These manipulators work the same way as ios member functions and flags. You can use more than one manipulator in a single statement.

Example:

Cout<<manip a<< manip b<< manip c<<item;

Cout<<manip a <<item1 <<manip b <<item2;

The above concatenation is great when you want to display data in column forms.

There are different types of manipulators you can use to alter fields. These manipulators include:

211

Manipulator	Set of Actions Performed	Alternative Member Function
Setw (int w)	Function for setting field with to w	Width()
Setprecision (int d)	Essential for setting the floating point numbers precision to d	Precision()
Setfill (int c)	Used to set the fill element with character c	Fill()
Setiosflags (long f)	Used for setting the format flag	Setf()
Resetiosflags (long f)	Used to clear any format flag specified by f	Unserf()
	Helps you insert a new line or to flush a stream.	"\n"

Example:

cout<<setw(8)<< 1234;

The above statement will print values 1, 2, 3,4 in a right justified field of 8 characters. The output of this statement can be altered to be left-justified. You can do this in the following way:

Cout<<setw (8) <<setiosflags (ios::left) <<1234;

File Operations

The I/O system handles file operations similar to the I/O operations. In this case, file streams are used as an interface between the specific files and the programs. Files have both input and output streams.

An input stream is a stream in which data is supplied to the program while an output stream is a stream that receives data from the program. The input stream extracts data from the file while the output stream enters data into the file. Any input operation used on the data acts as a link between the program and the input file. Similarly, output file operations consists of an output stream that links the program with the output file.

File Stream Classes

The input/output system in C++ programming language provides a set of stream classes essential for handling file methods and operations. Some of these methods include the use of **ifstream**, **ofstream**, and **fstream**.

File stream classes are derived from fstream base class which corresponds to the iostream class. The class for managing disk files should be declared in the fstream and the file should be included in every program that needs the use of the file.

Steps to File Operation

When using disk files you have to:

1. Select a suitable name for the file.

2. Define the data type and structure of the files.

3. Define the file purpose.

4. Define method for opening the files.

File Stream Classes

Class	Class contents
filebuf	This class sets the file buffers for read and write operation. The class has **Openprot** constant used in opening the file through the **open()** function. It also has both **open ()** and **close ()** member functions.

fstreambase	Fstreambase class offers various file operations common to the file streams. The fstreambase act as the base or super class for fstream, ifstream, and ofstream file operations. It also contains both **open()** and **close()** functions.
ifstream	It is responsible for input operations and has **open ()** as the default input mode. Ifstream inherits **get(), getline(),read(), tellg(),**and **seekg()** functions from the istream I/O system.
ofstream	Ofstream is responsible for output operation and it uses the **open()** with the default output mode. The class inherits function properties like **put(),write(), seekp(),** and **tellp()** from the ostream.
fstream	It is responsible for offering support for simultaneous I/O operations. It uses **open()** with its default input mode. Fstream inherits properties from istream and ostream classes via the iostream.

A filename consists of a string of characters making it a valid file name. A filename is divided into two parts: the primary name and an extension. For example, **file.doc, test.txt,** and **input.cpp** among other extensions.

To open any file, you have to create a file stream first and then link it to the filename. The file stream is declared using the ifstream, ofstream and fstream classes which are included in the **fstream** header file.

The file class created depends on the purpose for creation. That is, whether to read data or write data into the file.

After creation of the file, you can open it using:

1.   The constructor function in the class.

2.   The member function **open()** in the class.

Opening a file using constructor function is only applied when one file is being used in the stream, while the **open()** function method is used when opening multiple files using a single stream.

Opening Files Using Constructor

If a constructor is used to open a file, the filename initializes the file stream object. This can be achieved through:

1.   Creating a file stream object in order to manage the stream using an appropriate class. In this case, you can use ofstream class to create output stream while the ifstream class creates an input stream.

216

2. Using a desired filename so as to initialize the file object. For example, the following code is used to open a file named **performance** as an output:

> **ofstream outfile("performance");** // to display an output.

The outfile is created as an ofstream object whose main purpose is to manage the output stream.

You can also create an infile as an ifstream object and associate it with the file data for reading file inputs.

> **ifstream infile ("data");** // an input file

You can use the same file name to read or write data into a file.

When an object terminates, it automatically closes the connection to that file. In the above example on performance file, when the program is terminated, the performance file will be disconnected from the outfile stream. This also happens to the infile stream.

A filename consists of a string of characters making it a valid file name. A filename is divided into two parts: the primary name and an extension. For example, **file.doc, test.txt,** and **input.cpp** among other extensions.

To open any file, you have to create a file stream first and then link it to the filename. The file stream is declared using the ifstream, ofstream and fstream classes which are included in the **fstream** header file.

The file class created depends on the purpose for creation. That is, whether to read data or write data into the file.

After creation of the file, you can open it using:

1. The constructor function in the class.

2. The member function **open()** in the class.

Opening a file using constructor function is only applied when one file is being used in the stream while the **open()** function method is used when opening multiple file using a single stream.

Example: A program to write and read data from a file

```
#include <iostream.h>

#include <fstream.h>

int main()

{

char Prodname[20];

float price;

ofstream outfile("product");


cout <<"enter product's name:"
```

```
cin >>Prodname; outfile <<Prodname<<"\n";

cout <<"enter the product's price:";

cin >>price; outfile <<price <<"\n";

 outfile.close();


ifstream infile("product");

infile >>Prodname;

infile >>price;

cout <<"\n";

cout <<"Product name is : " << Prodname <<"\n";

cout <<"Product price: " << price <<"\n";


infile.close();

return 0;

}
```

// output

Product name is: Mango

Product price: 25

This program gets data via the input device like keyword and writes it to a file. After completion of the writing process, the file is closed. The file is then opened to read the information already written in the file and later displayed on the screen for the user to view.

Example 2: Writing to a file.

```cpp
#include <iostream>

#include <fstream>

using namespace std;


int main () {

  ofstream samplefile;

  samplefile.open ("sample.doc");

  samplefile << "Writing data to the sample.doc file.\n";

  samplefile.close();

  return 0;

}
```

Opening Files Using Open() Function

The **open()** function opens multiple files that use the same object stream. If a set of files are to be processed sequentially, then a single object stream is created to enable opening of each file.

Syntax

Void open (const char* filename, ios:: openmode mode);

or

open (filename, mode);

The first argument indicates the name of the file and file format together with its address, while the second part of the argument indicates the access mode of the file.

There are different access modes for opening a file, and they include:

File Mode	Description
in	It is the default mode for ifstream files. It opens the file for reading purposes.
Out	This mode is responsible for writing into a file. It is the default mode for ofstream.

221

binary	It is used to open a file in a binary form or mode.
App	The app mode is suitable for opening the file and appends the file outputs at the end.
Ate	This mode is responsible for opening the file and transferring the control to the end of the file.
Trunc	It is used to delete data from an existing file.
Nocreate	It tests the existence of a file and opens it if it exists.
Noreplace	If a file doesn't exist, noreplace opens a new file.

Example:

Fstream example_file;

Example_file.open(example.txt", ios::out);

In order to access the member function of fstream class, you have to create that class. **Example_file** is an object of type fstream. Calling the open() function allows you to open the file and write data into it.

The default open mode for the files are:

- ifstream ios::in

- ofstream ios::out

- fstream ios::in | ios::out

The symbol | is used to combine different modes. For example:

Example_file.open(example.txt", ios::out | ios::ate);

The input mode and control mode are combined to ensure the file is opened for writing then transfers the control to the end of the file.

When a program terminates, the allocated memory is freed up and all opened files are closed. Using the **close()** function ensures all the files are closed as soon as execution is complete.

With the stream insertion operator <<, you can write information into a file and use the stream extraction operator >> to read the information from the file.

Example: Opening a file using the open () and writing to the file

```
#include<iostream>

#include <fstream>

using namespace std;

int main()

{
```

```
fstream example_file;

example_file.open("example.doc", ios::out);

if(!example_file)

{

cout<<" File creation has failed";

}

else

{

cout<<"The new file was successfully created";

example_file<< "This is a new file created"; // writing to
the file

example_file.close(); // close the file to free memory

}

return 0;

}
```

//output

C:\users\Faith\Documents>notepad++   example.cpp   −o
example.exe

C:\users\Faith\Documents\example.doc

The new file was successfully created

C:\users\Faith\Documents>

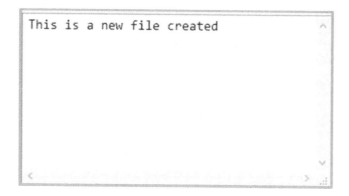

```
This is a new file created
```

In the above program, we have created an object example_file to be used in the fstream class. Then we open the object using the open() function and create a new file named example where to write data into. The file is assigned to out mode which allows writing into the file. If statement test whether the file exists or not if the file is unavailable "file creation has failed" statement is displayed, otherwise "The new file was successfully created" message will be displayed on the screen.

Example 2: Reading information from file

```
#include<iostream>

#include <fstream>

using namespace std;

int main()
```

```
{

fstream example_file;

example_file.open("example.doc", ios::in);

if(!example_file)

{

cout<<" The file doesn't exist";

}

else

{

Char ch;

While (!example.eof())

{example-file>>ch;

cout<<ch;}

example_file.close(); // close the file to free memory

}

return 0;

}
```

The above program reads the example.doc file we had already created in the previous example. To read a file, the **'in'** mode is used (ios::in). The extraction operator >> is used to print the file content of the file.

Finding End of File

When reading a file, it's important to determine the end of file, otherwise the program will be in an infinite loop if it doesn't detect the end of file. The programmer should provide appropriate instructions to the program so as to be able to detect the end of file.

When the end of file is determined, the reading data process can easily be terminated after all the data has been read. If the end-of-file is determined, the **fin** ifstream object will return a zero value if an error occurs in the file operation.

When the **fin** returns 0 after reaching the end-of-the-file, the while loop will terminate. You can also detect the end of file using the eof() function.

if(example.eof()!=0)

{exit file}

If the end-of-file is detected, a non-zero value is returned, otherwise if the end-of-file is not detected, a 0 value is returned. The program will automatically terminate after reaching the end-of-file.

File Pointers and Manipulators

Each C++ file has two pointers: input pointer and output pointer. The input pointer reads the content of a particular file location while the output pointer writes data to a given file location. Whenever an input or output file operation takes place, an appropriate pointer is updated automatically.

Default File Actions

When you open a file in a read-only mode, the input pointer is set at the start of the file so as to enable reading from the start of that file. If the file is opened in a write-only mode, all the file content is deleted and the output pointer is placed at the start of the file. This ensures that you write the file from the beginning point.

To add more data to an existing file, the file should be opened in an 'append' mode. This automatically moves the pointer to the end of the file.

Functions and Manipulations of File Pointer

All the actions and file operations using pointers take place by default. In order to control file pointer movement operations, there are various file stream classes you can use. Some of these file stream class member functions include:

- **seekg()** This function moves the (input) get pointer to a specific location.

- **Seekp()** The function moves the (output) put pointer to a specific location.

- **Tellg()** This function indicates the get pointer current position.

- **Tellp()** It indicates the put pointer current position.

Example:

infile.seekg(5);

This function will move the pointer to a number byte labelled 5 since the file bytes are numbered from 0. The pointer then points to the 6th byte which is the current location of the file.

Example 2:

ofstream myfile;

myfile.open("Welcome", ios::app);

int ppt=myfile.tellp();

When the above statements are executed, the output pointer moves up to the end of file "welcome" and the ppt value indicates the number of bytes in the file.

Specifying Offset Functions

The seek functions **(seekg()** and **seekp())** take two arguments:

- **Seekg** (offset, refposition)

- **Seekp** (offset,refposition)

The offset argument indicates the number of bytes to move the file pointer from the specified location by the refposition argument.

The refposition takes the form of:

- **ios::beg** this indicates the start of file.

- **ios::cur** indicates the current position of the pointer.

- **ios::end** this indicates the end of a file.

The **seekg()** function moves all the associated files with the get pointer. The **seekp()** moves the file and its associated files using the put pointer.

Pointer offset calls

Seek call	Action
fout.seekg(o,ios::beg)	Go to start
fout.seekg(o,ios::cur)	Stay at the current position
fout.seekg(o,ios::end)	Go to the end of file
fout.seekg(m,ios::beg)	Move to (m+1)th byte in the file
fout.seekg(m,ios::cur)	Go forward by m byte from current position
fout.seekg(-m,ios::cur)	Go backward by m bytes from current position.
fout.seekg(-m,ios::end)	Go backward by m bytes from the end

Sequential Input and Output Operations

There are a number of member functions for performing input and output file operations supported by file stream classes. The member functions **put()** and **get()**

handle single character operations at a time. The **write()** and **read()** functions write into and read to a block of binary data.

Put() and get() functions

You can write a single character into an associated stream using the **put()** function. The **get ()** function reads a single character from the associated stream. Let's write a program to illustrate how the functions works on a program.

```
#include <iostream.h>
#include <fstream.h>
#include<string.h>
int main()
{
char string[80]; cout<<"enter a string \n"; cin>>string;
int len =strlen(string);
fstream file;
file.open("TEXT". ios::in | ios::out); for (int i=o;i<len;i++) file.put(string[i]);
file .seekg(0); char ch; while(file)
{
file.get(ch);
cout<<ch;
}
return 0;
}
```

The above program requests for a string and once it receives the string, it writes on the file a character by character using the put () function with for loop. When the string length ends, the for loop is terminated.

After the execution, the program is displayed on the screen using the get() function. The get() function fetches a character by character data from the file until it reaches the end of file condition. The data read from the file is displayed on the screen for users to view using the << operator.

Write() and Read() Functions

The write () and read() function can handle binary forms of data. The data values are stored in the disk file using the same format used when they're being stored in an internal memory. For example, and int character can store 2 bytes of its data value into a binary form regardless of its size, while a 4 digit integer value can store 4 bytes in character form.

Binary input and output takes the form of:

```
infile.read (( char * ) & Var, sizeof (Var));

outfile.write (( char *) & Var, sizeof (Var));
```

The function receives two arguments: the address of the variable Var, and the length of the variable in the form of bytes. The address of the variable is represented with type char* (a pointer to a character data type).

Example:

```
#include <iostream.h>
#include <fstream.h>
#include <iomanip.h>
const char * filename ="Binary";
int main()
{

float weight[4] ={ 175.5,153.0,167.25,160.70};
ofstream outfile;
outfile.open(myfile);
outfile.write((char *) & weight, sizeof(weight));
outfile.close();
for (int j=0;j<4;j++)
weight[j]=0; ifstream infile; infile.open(myfile);
infile.read ((char *) & weight, sizeof (weight));
for (j=0;j<4;j++)
{
cout.setf(ios::showpoint);
cout<<setw(10)<<setprecision(2)<<weight[j];
} infile.close(); return 0;
}
```

Error Handling During File Operation

When carrying out various file operations, there are various errors encountered. Some of these problems encountered include:

- Non-existence of the file you are trying to access.

- The file name being used to create a new file already exists.

- Attempting an invalid file operation like trying to read data past the end of file condition.

233

- Not enough memory in the disk drive to store more data.

- Dealing with an invalid file name.

These are some of the common file operation problems you may face when handling and manipulating files. File operation stream in C++ language inherits the '**stream-state**' member from the ios class.

The stream-state member keeps information on the status of the current opened file. The ios class support a number of member functions for reading the file status recorded on the stream.

Error handling functions

Function	Meaning and its Return Value
Eof()	Eof() returns a true value or a non-zero value if the end of file is successfully detected while reading the file, otherwise, it will return a zero value.
Fail()	This functions returns true after the failure of both input and output operations.
Bad()	If an attempt of an invalid operation is encountered or unrecoverable error, it returns true. If the error can be recovered and file

	operation continues, then it returns false value
Good()	If no error has been encountered, it will return true. If the file.good() function returns true, then you can continue with other I/O operations. If it returns false, there are no further operations are carried out.

Chapter Summary

Input/output streams are an important feature in C++ programming language. The streams help in class definition and provide a set of library functions that perform a series of functions. In this chapter, you learned about the C++ streams concept and how to use input and output stream to execute programs. You also learned the various devices you can use when working with various stream input and outputs. C++ stream classes will enable you to:

- Define a hierarchy of classes that defines the use of streams console unit and the disk files.

- Learn how to declare the I/O stream classes in the header file as well as learn the various console operations using the stream classes.

- Learn different types of class names and their properties and functionalities.

235

- Learn how ios class provide basic support for I/O operations on both unformatted i/o operation and formatted i/o operations.

- Use the overloaded operators (>>&<<) used for data inputs and outputs. The **cin** standard library functions use the overloaded operators >> to read data from an input device. While **cout** standard library function operator << is used to display data on the screen or output device.

- Use unformatted I/O operations like **put()** and **get()** functions. The **put()** function is a member of ostream class which is used to output data character by character, while the **get()** function works as input stream.

- Learn how to use getline () and write() functions.

- Learn various formatted console I/O operations supported by C++ language to format the output.

- Use ios class functions and flags to format data inputs.

- How to use user-defined output functions or the use of output manipulators and other formatting features of ios class functions to format the output.

- Learn how to use user-defined functions to format output.

- Learn how to manage output with manipulators.

- Perform various file operations and know how to handle stream classes.

- Know how to open files using constructors and using **open ()** function, create new files and how to write into a file.

- Use C++ to write a code on how to open a file, write a code of how to write into an existing file or creating a new file, as well as write a code of reading information from a file.

- Use the close () member function which is added in every file code to close the file.

- Learn how to control input output streams through the use of classes. Both istream and ostream control the input and output functions.

- Using working examples, derive an iostream class from the istream and ostream classes. Other classes derived in I/O streams include: **istream_withassigh.ostream_withassign** and **iostream_withassign**. These classes are derived from the properties of istream, ostream, and iostream classes respectively.

- Use **eof ()** function to test whether the end of file is reached and it returns value 1 if it's detected. You're able to write a code that determines the end-of-file, how to use the close() function to terminate a program, and use of pointers to manipulate files.

237

- Use **seekg()** function links to the associated file pointer (both input and output file pointer).

- Write codes using the put() and get() functions which reads and writes a single character in a file while the write() and read() are used for writing and reading a block of binary data.

- Know how to how to handle errors during file operations.

In the next chapter you will learn about exception handling. By the end of the chapter, you will understand the concept and principles of exception handling, mechanisms of exception handling, and the use of throw and catch exceptions mechanisms.

Chapter Nine:
Exception Handling

Introduction

Exception handling provides you with a way to create and deal with the errors that occur during the program development process, such as run time errors. This is achieved by transferring the control of the program to a special function called **handlers.**

During the program development process, there are cases where the programmer is uncertain whether a piece of code will run successfully or not due to run time errors like limited resource allocation or out of range errors.

To solve this problem, you have to place the piece of code under the exception inspection. This is achieved by enclosing the piece of code in a try block. When an exceptional circumstance arises within that block of code, then an exception is thrown that transfers the control to the exception handler.

If there are no exception detected or thrown, then the program code continues to execute normally and the handlers created are ignored.

When the program code encounters an exceptional condition, it's important to identify the exception and deal with it effectively. An exception is that part of an object that occurs whenever an error is encountered on that part of the program.

Principles of Exception Handling

Exception handling is a mechanism for detecting and reporting exceptional circumstances in a program to ensure an appropriate action is implemented. Exception handling mechanism involves:

1. Detecting the exceptions (problem).

2. Throwing the exception (acknowledge the error has occurred).

3. Catching the exception (Receive detail information on the error).

4. Handling the exceptions (Taking corrective actions to solve the problem).

An exception handling mechanism should have two segments: one segment to detect the error and throw exceptions while the other segment will catch the exceptions and take up appropriate measures to handle the errors.

There are two types of exceptions; **Synchronous** and **asynchronous** exceptions. **Synchronous** exceptions are encountered during program run-time due to program anomalies, and they include out of range index error and overflow error. Occurrence of events beyond the program control results in **asynchronous** exceptions. An example of **asynchronous** exceptions is keyboard interrupts.

Exception Handling Mechanisms

Exception handling is built on three keyword operators:

1. Try.

2. Throw.

3. Catch.

The try keyword prefaces a block of statements in order to generate exceptions. The block of statements is known as the try block. Once an exception is detected it is thrown using the throw keyword inside the try block statements. Exception handlers are defined by the use of the catch keyword that catches an exception thrown using the throw statement in the try block. The catch block statements must appear immediately after the try block.

Syntax

```
Try

{

//block of statements to be tried

Throw exception

}

Catch (type arguments)

{
```

Code to be executed in case of exception

```
}
```

When an exception is thrown in the try block, the program control is transferred from the try block into the catch statement. If the thrown object type matches the arguments type in the catch block, then the catch statements to handle exceptions is executed.

If the object arguments don't match, the program is aborted using abort () function. if no exception is detected or thrown, then the control is taken back immediately using the catch block.

Example:

```
#include <iostream.h>

using namespace std;

int main()

{

  try

  {

    throw 15;

  }

  catch(int a)

  {
```

```
    cout<< "An exception has occurred"; <<endl;

}

return 0;

}
```

If there is no exception thrown, the catch statements will not be executed.

Example:

```cpp
# include <iostream>
using namespace std;
void divide (int x,int y,int z)
 {
    cout<<"we are outside the function";
    if ( ( x-y) != 0)
     {
       int r=z/(x-y);
        cout<<"result = "<<r;
     }
     else
      {
        throw(x-y);
      }
 }
int main()
{
try

cout<<"we are inside the try block";
divide(10,20,30);
divide(10,10,20);
}

catch (int i)
{
cout<<"caught the exception";
}
return 0;
}
```

// output

We are outside the try block We are inside the function Result =-3

We are inside the function

Caught the exception

Throw Mechanism

When an exception is detected, it is thrown using the following command:

```
throw (exception); throw exception; throw;
```

The exception object thrown may be of any form, even constants. Other objects not intended for error handling can also be thrown. If an exception is thrown, a catch statement will be able to catch it. The program control will be transferred from the try block into the catch block.

Catching Mechanisms

The exception handler will have a code in the catch block. The catch block is a function on its own and it's used to manage exceptions.

```
Catch(type arg)
{   statements for managing exceptions
}
```

The type is used to indicate the type of exception handled by the catch block. The arguments are optional. The catch statement catches exceptions with type that matches the catch parameter. After the exception is caught, the block code inside the catch block is executed. When the handler is executed, the control is passed immediately. If the catch statements doesn't catch the exception then the catch block statements will be skipped.

245

Chapter Summary

Exceptions are various errors a program may encounter during its running time. C++ programming language has a built-in language function for trapping all program errors and control exceptions. The latest C++ compiler supports this feature making it easy for the user to debug a program.

- An exception acts as an object which is sent from the part of the program where an error has occurred to the part of the program where the error will be controlled.

- Exception method is done via the use of three keywords: try, throw and catch. The try keyword is for detecting an exception in the file and the exception statements known as try block is enclosed within curly braces.

- The catch block receives the exception sent by the throwing block inside the try block.

- You can create multiple catch blocks within a program or even pass the exception to another exception handler.

- Specified exceptions are great for binding functions to throw only condition for a specified exception.

Final Words

C++ programming language is a competitive general purpose program which borrows some features of imperative programming paradigm and can run on any platform. It is referred to as an imperative programming language because it uses step by step processes in order to achieve its goals. The program uses the concept of object oriented program to design and implement complex programs.

The program revolves around data which is created using objects. These objects communicate with each other by passing messages. The objects don't have to know the detail information of another object so as to exchange data between them. They only need to establish a connection between themselves and exchange information.

C++ programming language utilizes the features of OOP paradigms to develop and execute a program. Some of these features include: use of objects, classes, data abstractions and encapsulation, inheritance and polymorphism.

The program focuses on the use of data rather than procedures to solve real world problems. The program tries to eliminate the shortcomings of other conventional programming languages by improving the data security of programs, promoting code reusability and its ability to use inheritance feature to make an effective program.

Just like many other OOP languages, C++ supports various building blocks. In this tutorial, you have learned how to use various built-in data types when handling simple to complex programs. The data types are divided into primitive data types, derived data types, and abstract data types. You not only learned how to use the primitive or standard data types, but also how to declare your own user-defined datatypes.

You learned how to create arrays for storing values, and how you can access variables created using arrays. You also learned how to initialize arrays and how to work with different types of arrays.

Pointers play an important role in the allocation of memory space to the user programs. When declaring variables, a memory space is allocated for the variable. Each variable has a defined memory address for accessing the variable. Therefore, in this tutorial, you learned how to create programs that assign the memory address to the pointer variable. You also learned how to use dynamic free store operators like new and delete operator to allocate and deallocate memory space. The computer memory is a limited resource, therefore, you have to free the memory when a program no longer needs it and allocate that memory space to another program that needs it.

You also learned how to use library functions and user-defined functions in developing programs. The library functions are pre-defined or built-in C++ functions which perform a number of tasks. C++ also allow users to define their own functions and write a block of statements to be executed once the function is invoked. In this tutorial, you learned how to create your own function,

function definition and declaration. You are also able to learn how to call functions and pass parameters to a function. You're able to know how to use function prototype, and use inline functions in a program.

Another important feature you learned about is how to organize different data elements and variables into a single unit using structures. You learned how to initialize a structure element, how to access the structure memory and how to use references.

In chapters two and three, you learned the basic concepts in OOP and how to work with classes and objects. You're now able to define a class and declare class members either private, public, or protected. Defining the class header files will allow you to reuse the code in various files. The class definition is put in a header file with the same name as the class. The member functions are stored outside the class and stored with the same name as the class.

You are now able to create class objects and define both private and public access specifiers, define data members and member functions, and use protected data members. C++ presents different types of class member functions which can be utilized to manipulate data. Learning how to use each of the data members will make it easy to modify data files and make calls to the member functions.

Classes can be created in two forms in C++ programming language: using a base class or using a derived class. The base class allows you to build other classes from it while a derived class inherits the properties and characteristics of the base class. You're now able to create a base class and derived class and extend the class functionality using overriding members.

In chapter 4, we discussed inheritance. That is, how to derive a new class from an existing class. In inheritance, a class borrows the members of other classes so as to avoid any repetitions. When inheriting members, the public members of the base class will remain public while the protected members will remain protected, while the private members will remain private in the derived class.

There are different types of inheritance users can define and these include: single inheritance, multiple inheritance, hierarchical inheritance, multi-level inheritance, and hybrid inheritance.

You are now able to create objects using constructors and destructors of derived objects. The constructors will help in initializing member variables while the destructor will destroy the object and free up memory space.

During a program execution, the compiler automatically calls for the constructor and destructor variables. Constructors and destructors can be used in the base class and also in the derived class. When the constructor is used in the derived class, the arguments will be passed to the base class.

Upcasting is another feature which utilizes the use of base class reference or a pointer to point directly to a subclass. In this chapter, you are able to learn how to use upcasting and downcasting features to create a base class.

C++ allows you to dynamically allocate memory space to programs. You can allocate the memory space to a program by initially defining the program variables before the program executes. In such a case, the memory is determined during run-time or based on the user inputs. Dynamically, allocation is achieved through the use of new and delete operators.

The new operator followed by the data type specifier automatically allocates memory space to the file. It allows you to allocate memory to an array of elements using the new[] operator. The delete operator deallocates the memory thus making the memory available for other programs When dealing with multiple elements the delete [] operator is used to deallocate memory space. If you create a memory and forget to delete it, it creates a memory leak. therefore, any memory created on the heap should be freed when no longer in use to avoid creating a memory leak.

Polymorphism is an OOP feature that enables you to have an object with more than one form. Creating multiple inheritance in a class results in polymorphism. Polymorphism is divided into two: run-time polymorphism and compile time polymorphism. Run-time polymorphism is achieved by use of overloading functions and virtual functions, while compile time polymorphism is achieved via overriding function and operator overloading. You now have practical knowledge about how to create virtual functions, overloading functions, and

251

overriding functions. You also learned how to access the private member function in a derived class using virtual keyword and how to create abstract classes and pure virtual functions.

In chapter six, we discussed how constructors and destructors work, characteristics of constructors, how to define and declare a constructor class, and working with different types of constructors. We also discussed in class destructor and how to declare a class destructor.

Templates allows functions and classes to use generic type. This plays an important role on how functions and classes work by allowing users to define different data types without the need of rewriting the code. A template allows you to create a generic class which supports any data type. There are two main types of templates: function templates and class templates.

A class template works like a normal class with a prefix 'template' followed by the class identifier. Class templates accept members with any type of arguments. These templates are mostly used in implementing containers.

You can also create a derived class from the class template through a process known as instantiation. The derived class is known as template class. You can also pass multiple parameters to a class template. A multiple parameter class template supports more than one generic data type. The generic type classes are separated by commas.

Function templates accommodate multiple data types compared to the normal function which only accommodates a single data type. Templates allow you to overload a normal function with different data types. This makes them more useful since you only have to write a single program that can work with all data types. In this tutorial, you learned to create templates with multiple parameters, how to use overloading template functions and how to create member function templates.

This programming language supports a lot of libraries which are used in performing the input and output functions. The input output operations are performed using a series of bytes known as streams. This chapter discusses the input output streams used in running the program effectively. A stream acts as a sequence of bytes forming the source and destination of input output data. The source stream supplies data to a program through the use of an input device while the destination stream is used to receive an output from the program.

Input/output operations are implemented through the use of streams concepts and stream classes. These stream classes are declared in the header file of the iostream. C++ stream classes act as a logical device that accepts data inputs and displays output. Streams are I/O operations which can work in any device. The streams acts as both the source and the destination.

Stream classes consists of a hierarchy of classes which define streams for handling the system console unit and the disk files. Stream classes perform both input and output operations. The ios class is the base class for the input stream while ostream acts as the output stream. There are different class streams you can use to manipulate your files.

Overloaded operators >> and << are used for both input and output operations. The input operator >> uses the standard cin library to access input data. The output operator << is used together with cout to display the content. The >> operator is overloaded in an istream while << is overloaded in an ostream.

You can define the put () and get() functions to handle input/output operations on a single character. Other functions which can be used to handle class streams include the use of getline() and write () functions. Line oriented I/O functions like getline() and write() helps you to easily read and write into a line of text.

The header file iomanip provides a wide set of standard function manipulators which manipulate an output format. There are also various format consoles you can use to format data output. These formatted consoles include the use of ios class function and flags or the use of user-defined functions. You also learned about various file operations and using file stream classes.

The file operations work similarly to the console I/O operations. Some of the file operations you now understand are how to open files, write files, read from files, and close a file. When opening files, you can use constructors or use open () function. The file open() function works within a set of file stream classes like fstreambase, ifstream, and ofstream. The eof() function is used to detect the end of the file. When the end of file is detected the program is terminated.

Each file created has two types of pointers: the input pointer and the output pointer. The input file pointer reads the contents of the file while the output pointer is used to write into the file. whenever an I/O operation takes places, the specific file pointer is activated automatically. There are also various functions you can use to manipulate file pointers like the seekg() function. Other functions used to manipulate files include write() and read() function which write and read a block of binary data while put() and get() functions are used to read and write a single character.

Lastly, you learned how to handle errors during file operations and how to handle exceptions in a program. The exception handling mechanism involves use of three keywords: try, throw and catch exceptions to allow to detect anomalies, throw exceptions, and come up with appropriate measures to handle the exceptions.

References

http://www.cplusplus.com/doc/tutorial/dynamic/

https://codescracker.com/cpp/cpp-data-structures.htm

https://www.edureka.co/blog/dynamic-memory-allocation-cpp/

https://www.edureka.co/blog/inline-function-in-cpp/

https://www.geeksforgeeks.org/c-classes-and-objects/

https://www.geeksforgeeks.org/object-oriented-programming-in-cpp/

https://www.programiz.com/cpp-programming/function

https://www.softwaretestinghelp.com/data-structures-in-cpp/

https://www.studytonight.com/cpp/function-overriding.php

https://www.studytonight.com/cpp/order-of-constructor-call.php

https://www.studytonight.com/cpp/types-of-member-function.php

https://www.tutorialspoint.com/cplusplus/cpp_arrays.htm

https://www.w3schools.in/cplusplus-tutorial/constructors-destructors/

Image Credit: geeksforgeeks.com

Image Credit: studytonight.com

Made in United States
North Haven, CT
23 April 2022

18474707R10143